BAR BRITISH SERIES 648 | 2019

INSCRIBED VERVELS

*A corpus and discussion of
late medieval and Renaissance
hawking rings found in Britain*

MICHAEL LEWIS
AND IAN RICHARDSON

BAR
PUBLISHING

Published in 2019 by
BAR Publishing, Oxford

BAR British Series 648

Inscribed Vervels

ISBN 978 1 4073 1678 9 paperback
ISBN 978 1 4073 5520 7 e-format

COVER IMAGE *Vervel from Princes Risborough (BH-D528FA).*
Image courtesy of the Portable Antiquities Scheme.

BAR
PUBLISHING

BAR titles are available from:

BAR Publishing
122 Banbury Rd, Oxford, OX2 7BP, UK
EMAIL info@barpublishing.com
PHONE +44 (0)1865 310431
FAX +44 (0)1865 316916
www.barpublishing.com

Acknowledgements

We would very much like to thank all those who have found, researched and recorded the vervels catalogued in this book, in particular the local Finds Liaison Officers of the Portable Antiquities Scheme, museum curators at the British Museum and local museums, and also many other experts (we have sought to acknowledge this in the records below).

We are grateful to the British Museum for funding access to research material and for funding a 'vervels workshop' and to those who gave their time to attend: Steven Ashley (Norfolk County Council), Clive Cheesman (College of Arms), Lloyd de Beer (British Museum), Leigh Holmes (The Hawking Centre), Dora Thornton (The Goldsmiths Company) and Ross Turle (Hampshire Cultural Trust). Much useful insight and information was garnered at this meeting. Also, to Laura Greer from The Hawking Centre and to Stella, the Harris hawk whom Laura brought along on the day to demonstrate for us all a bird in flight!

The British Museum also supported our trips to Valkenswaard, Netherlands, to meet Jac van Geert of the Museum of Falconry, and to Norwich Castle Museum, where we were able to inspect what we believe is the largest public collection of vervels in the country, under the curatorship of Tim Pestell.

Thanks are due to Laura Perucchetti and her colleagues Antony Simpson, Duncan Hook and Andrew Meek in the British Museum Department of Scientific Research for analysing the vervels in the Museum's collection, and to colleagues in the British Museum's Department of Britain, Europe and Prehistory for making these vervels available to us.

We also are grateful to Kirstin Kennedy, formerly of the Victoria & Albert Museum, who kindly gave us access to the vervels in their collection, and to Emma Raphael from Raphael Historic Falconry, who passed on much useful information in the early stages of our project.

We would especially like to thank Margaret Broomfield who kindly commented on the text, Eljas Oksanen who helped with GIS distribution maps, and Janina Parol for image manipulation throughout the document. All existing errors remain our own.

Contents

Preface

This book provides a corpus of inscribed hawking rings (vervels) reported Treasure via the Portable Antiquities Scheme (PAS) over the last twenty years, that is since the implementation of the Treasure Act 1996 (in September 1997) until the end of 2017.

In the 'introduction' there are various figures, graphs and tables, which are listed below. In the 'catalogue' that follows, the vervels are listed by country (England or Wales), then alphabetically by county, then findspot. At the end of each entry there is an image of the vervel in question, as well as any associated figures. It is important to note that these images have been photographed by various people across the country, so we have tried to make these images consistent in appearance, but that has not always been possible.

List of Figures, Graphs, Maps and Tables

Tables

Maps

Introduction

Vervels (alternatively spelt *vervils*, *varvels* or *vervailles*, but pronounced 'var-vels'),[1] also known as hawking rings, are not common finds, but small numbers are reported every year under the Treasure Act 1996 via the Portable Antiquities Scheme (PAS) – a project to record archaeological finds made by the public to advance knowledge. All the inscribed vervels found in recent years (and catalogued below) have been found by metal-detector users and this contribution of metal-detecting (and the Scheme itself) to further our knowledge of Britain's past is well attested (Lewis 2016: 131).

Inscribed vervels are a fascinating find type since they may contain small, but important, amounts of personal information relating to the owners of the hunting birds to which these items were once attached. This book is not only a corpus of vervel-finds made over the last 20 years, but explores the use and function of these objects, their form, construction and typology, chronology and distribution.

It is generally said that vervels connected the leather jesses attached to a hawk's legs to its leash, used in training and to tie the bird to its perch or block (Latham 1614). However (and as discussed further below), some might have been worn on the bird's foot, much like modern identification rings used by pigeon fanciers and conservationists, as well as falconers. Whatever their practical application, inscribed vervels had an additional function, principally to denote the ownership of hunting birds (Parker 1894), presumably in case they were lost: this use is clearly apparent upon a silver vervel (**B18**) found near Taunton, Somerset, which has the inscribed command 'RETOURNE TOO // HVGH PORTMAN'. Given the nature of hawking, necessitating a close understanding between the falconer and his bird, the loss of one would have been noticed immediately and missing creatures would have been searched for; nowadays GPS devices and radio transmitters (which were obviously not used in the past) help track lost birds.

The acquisition, training and keeping of hunting birds made them expensive investments, and there were legal requirements for those who found a lost bird to return it or recompense its owner (Grassby 1997: 48). This would have only been possible if the bird retained one (or more) of its vervels for identification, and the longer it was in the wild, the less likely this would have been; Sir Thomas Sherley (1603), for example, complains of a hawk being lost for two days, after being seemingly caught up in a tree

by its vervels (ironically in place to ensure its safe return) – the bird gnawed at his jesses, made wet in the rain, until releasing the stitches which held the vervels [note plural] in place. Although it seems most likely that the vervels found today are from lost birds, or perhaps lost whilst birds were hunting, it is also possible that they were dropped when falconers changed out equipment in the field, a practice still common (Emma Raphael: *pers. comm*).

Most of the vervels found over the last 20 years date from the late 16th and 17th centuries (see below), although medieval examples have been recorded: of note is a vervel probably associated with Edward V (r.1483), as Prince of Wales, found at Eaton Bray, Bedfordshire (**A01**). During the Middle Ages an array of hunting birds were flown, especially falcons (such as peregrines, lanners, kestrels, merlins and hobbies), goshawks and sparrowhawks. The *Book of St Albans* (1486) gives the social rank needed to own birds of prey, suggesting an element of control over who hunted and with what, but the extent to which this tome reflects contemporary reality might have been somewhat different. By the 17th century, when falconry again flourished, it was common for gentlemen to fly falcons and hawks. Those paid for by the Duke of Bedford between 1660 and 1671, for example, included goshawks, lanner falcons, a Nova Scotia hawk, an Irish falcon, brook hawks and Scotch hawks (Thomson 1940: 228-9). The popularity of firearms, new breeds of hunting dogs and a preference for other rural pursuits, as well as the enclosure of much open countryside, all contributed to a rapid decline in the sport of falconry in Britain from the early 18th century (Grassby 1997: 60-2). Although the late 18th and 19th centuries saw the establishment and dissolution of clubs for a small number of wealthy participants, falconry was changing. The British Falconers' Club, founded in 1927 (and still in existence) represented falconry's evolution into a hobby practiced mostly by amateur enthusiasts. As noted earlier, modern materials enable birds to carry lightweight identity tags slipped onto jesses and some are fitted with radio transmitters to aid in their recovery (Glasier 1998, 16ff, 84, 213). So, as the practice of falconry has developed so has the equipment used by falconers.

Historical Context

Falconry is an activity where its chief asset is, by its very nature, prone to becoming lost – birds of prey can be tamed through training, but they are not domesticated animals. It is almost inevitable that 'sooner or later' falconers lose a hawk, but 'most often this is the result of using faulty equipment, or just plain carelessness on the falconer's

---

[1] Varvel or vervel derives from the Old French for *vervelle* (Falcon's leg fetter), from the Latin *vetibulum* (joint) (Morel & Horobin 2018: 3).

part' (Glasier 1998: 208). It makes sense that measures have long been taken to enable the owner of a lost bird to be identified and the hawk returned. A small ring, bearing the basic details of the owner and attached by some means to the bird, has been employed for this purpose from at least the Middle Ages and continues to this day in the use of anodized metal bands, slipped around a bird's foot when they are less than a week old (Leigh Holmes, *pers. comm.*).

Documentary evidence for the use of vervels comes to us from three primary types of sources: contemporary treatises and historic synopsis on the sport of falconry, administrative documents (inventories, accounts and records), and artistic representations.

Contemporary Treatises and Historic Synopsis

Falconry has a longstanding and extensive literary tradition. James Hartin's (1891) *Bibliotheca Acciptraria: a catalogue of books ancient and modern relating to falconry* provides a thorough summary of treatises, books and manuscripts from the 13th century to his own time, including Russian, Middle Eastern and Far Eastern sources, as well as those from Western Europe. One of the most-acclaimed books on the subject, the Holy Roman Emperor Frederick II's *De Arte Venandi cum Avibus* (the Art of Hunting with Birds), written between 1241 and 1245, describes the use of vervels in some detail, even if they are not mentioned by name:

> 'Two rings or two stitches of cuirass, no matter whether they are of iron, bronze or horn, will be fit. The unperforated end of the jesses, which must hang down at the back of the feet [of the bird], will be inserted into the ring and the portion of the strap that will pass through this ring will be folded and sewn to the rest of the strap, [so that it] will not have crossed the ring, or it will be knotted...' (Frederick II: see Wood & Fyfe 1943: 139-40; Morel & Horobin 2018: 8).

Adelard of Bath (c.1080-c.1152) describes the use of vervels in his *Treatises on Birds*, saying that the bird's jesses may be attached to a single flat ring (246-7, following Oggins 2004: 24). Intriguing is the fact that neither source refers to these 'rings' – presumably Type A (washer) vervels (see classification below) – being inscribed; perhaps it was so obvious that vervels would have been marked in some way to identify the bird's owner that both commentators neglect to mention it.

A mid-to-late 18th century *L'Encyclopédie* (Diderot & D'Alembert 1751-72) not only describes Type A vervels but also illustrates them (see more below):

> *'petits anneaux de cuivre que l'on met aux pies des oiseaux à des lanieres de cuir, avec lesquelles on les tient sur le poing. Sur ces anneaux est gravé, d'un coté, Je suis au Roi, et de l'autre, le nom du commandant de la fauconnerie'* (small copper rings that are tied to the feet of birds with leather straps [jesses] and then held in the fist. On these rings is inscribed on one side 'I am of the King' and on the other, the name of the chief falconer).

Of note is the fact that these are described as being made of copper, whereas all those listed in the catalogue below (apart from **A03**) are precious metal. Perhaps it is possible that base-metal vervels were more commonly used in continental Europe than in England. Of further interest, is the fact that the expression 'I am of the King' in *L'Encyclopédie* (Fig. 1) is similar to that found on a gold vervel in the British Museum (1855,1201.217; Fig. 2), which is inscribed on one side (in Latin) *'sum regis anglie'*, though this inscription is not found on any vervels in the catalogue below of recent finds.

Some sources describe vervels as being rings, but are not specific about whether these are flat – and therefore Type A vervels (as described above) – or with high sides – and therefore more likely to be of Type B (if not also attached to a shield; see classification below). Type B (ring) vervels seem to be described amongst the gifts to guests during the fifth course at a banquet celebrating the marriage of Duke Lionel of Clarence and Violanti Visconti (1368), listed as 'six peregrine falcons, with hoods of velvet, having pearls on top, and buttons and rings...of silver' (Oggins 2004: 111).

Similarly, it is noted is that during the reign of Edward I (r.1272-1307), Geoffrey le Falconer 'held nine acres and a messuage in Great Linton, Cambridgeshire, by rendering yearly six pairs of jesses with varvels...' (following Oggins 2004: 155, n.63). Of note here is the fact that vervels were prized, no doubt because most appear (from the evidence we have) to be made of precious metals.

David Dalby's (1965) *Lexicon of the Medieval German Hunt: a lexicon of Middle High German Terms (1050-1500)* provides evidence of the use of small escutcheons bearing the arms of a birds' owner. These *schildechin* (Cummings 2001: 201) are likely to be Type C (ring with shield) vervels, which are described in accounting records (see below).

The late 16th and 17th centuries saw an increase in the number of publications on falconry (Hartin, 1891: 1-35), and therefore those that mention vervels. Antoine Furetière's (1690) *Dictionnaire universel* is fairly generic in its description of hawking rings, saying that a vervel was 'a small ring or plate, attached to the feet of the bird of prey, where there is an imprint of the arms of the lord to whom it belongs, or some other mark that makes it recognisable'. This need is made clear in a mid-19th century work – *Beiträge zur Geschichte der Jagd und der Falknerei in Deutschland* – reporting on an incident in July 1648 when Marshal Bodo von Hodenberg was able to attribute a lost falcon to William VI, Landgrave of Hessen-Kassel (1629-63), because of the silver rings bearing the 'Hessian Lion' and the letters W.L.Z.H.

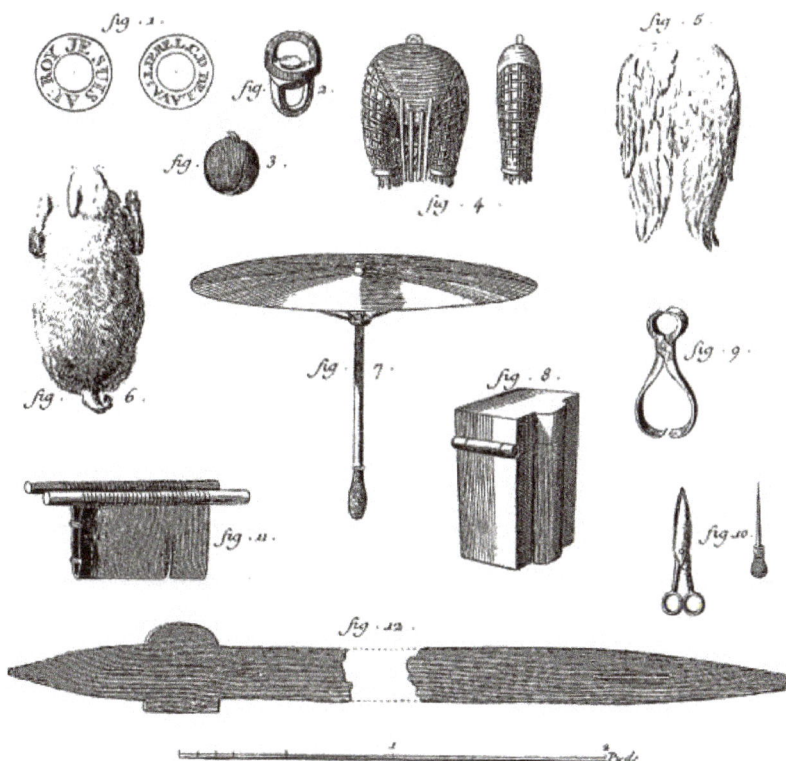

Fig. 1: Vervels and hawking equipment in *L'Encyclopédie Chasses Pêches*.

Fig. 2: Gold vervel in the British Museum (1855,1201.217), inscribed 'sum regis anglie' (© The Trustees of the British Museum).

(Landau 1849: 339). The use of vervels is also discussed, and in some detail, by George Turberville (1611: 140) who wrote:

> 'then also put on her Iesses, the which must bee of Shameuse, leather, or soft calues leather, or such other leather as may bée gentle and playable to her legge. At the end therof, it shall not bée amisse to sette *two Veruelles of Siluer*, the one thereof may haue the Armes of the King, or Quéen whom you serue, and the other a Scutcheon of your owne arms. For as much as when they flee out, if they chance to be taken vp, they may the sooner be retourned againe, and re|stored to their owners, the which you must then remember to rewarde the taker vp of his hawk liberally. You shall also put her on a paire of good belles...' [sic].

Here the implied use of two vervels together is of particular interest, with one having the arms of the monarch and the other having the owner's personal arms. The catalogue below gives examples of several inscribed (Type C) vervels that have upon them the arms of either a member of the nobility or the ruling monarch, suggesting that this discourse of the early 17th century reflects a practice that was once current, especially in the mid-late 16th and early 17th centuries based on the date of the vervels that have been recovered through metal-detecting. Of note in this regard is also a Type C vervel from Colney, Norfolk (**Ciii05**) that shows upon it (but on either side of the same shield) the arms of Charles Brandon, 1st Duke of Suffolk (d.1545), and the Tudor Royal arms.

How these vervels were affixed to the legs of hunting birds is uncertain (see discussion below), as the rings of Type B and some Type C vervels can be quite small. Some insight is perhaps provided by *La fauconnerie de Charles d'Arcussia de Capré* (1615: 10) which recommends putting bells and vervels on to *niaises* (young birds taken from the nest) early on in their training, which might imply that young birds were prone to wander, but may also suggest ringing birds of a young age was more practical (as outlined below).

Distinct from the vervels discussed above is a type described by Sir Thomas Sherley (1603), who wrote of his experiments in an alternative form of vervel called the 'garter'. Here it is stated that these were attached around a bird's leg, rather than to its jesses. Type D vervels (see classification below) are incredibly rare, and therefore may not have gained popular use.

Administrative Records

Legislation in Britain regarding the returning of birds to their owners dates from at least the Middle Ages. The Finding of Hawks Act, passed by the English Parliament of 1361, made it a felony to steal a manned bird. Somewhat confusingly, under Common Law, 'no wild creature could be private property', so a lost hawk belonged to whoever reclaimed it, even when it was wearing identification rings (Grassby 1997: 48). This does imply that vervels were regularly in use by the High Middle Ages and that anyone finding a bird of prey with hawking rings attached understood their import. It might also be deduced that anyone finding a hawk belonging to an aristocrat might return it, fearing it might be more trouble than it is worth not to, and also hopeful of receiving a reward.

These principles are reinforced by later laws. In the reign of Henry VIII (r.1509-47), regarding the failure to return lost hawks of the King (31 Hen VIII, c.12), and by the Scottish Parliament, under James VII (r.1685-8; James II in England) – 'an Act against stealing of dogs and hawks' ordained that 'whomsoever hereafter shall steal a hawk out of its nest or eyrie...or vervel from a hawk, with the master's name or style thereon, shall be fine in the sum of 500 merks Scot' (1685/4/48).

Also described in some medieval accounts are vervels consisting of rings with heraldic shields attached (Type C vervels). The accounts of the Duke of Burgundy (dated 29 August 1368) record that Philip the Bold paid Vincant de Couloigne, a goldsmith of Paris, 14 Francs 'for the gold for, and fabrication of, two vervels and a golden tore [swivel], enamelled with the arms of monsignor, for the good heron hawk' (Morel & Horobin 2018: 8). Another order by the Duke of Burgundy (this time in 1421) says that an order was sent to Jehan de Zeelanden, a goldsmith resident in Ghent, for 'seven dozen or swivels and vervels of gold and silver enamel to bear the name and arms of Monseigneur for his hawks' (ibid.). Similarly, Marie de Clèves (1426-87), Duchess of Orleans and mother of the future King Louis XII, had, in 1455, fourteen vervels of silver-gilt bearing her motto made for her hawks; indeed, in 1474 she ordered similar for her dogs – 'copper emblems of the monseigneur's arms and of madam, to attach the necklaces of the whippets or windhounds' (ibid).

The popularity of falconry among the English nobility and landed gentry during the 16th and 17th centuries meant individuals often each owned a number of birds, resulting in considerable requisitioning of all of the supplies necessary to maintain them and have them ready for flying.

As such, vervels are among the items that are listed in contemporary inventories and correspondence. Inventories of the possessions at the palaces, houses and hunting lodges associated with Henry VIII, for example reveal a considerable amount of falconry material, including at Westminster (for example) nine 'vervells of silver with the kings Armes' and four 'vervelles of Silver for hawkes'

(following MacGregor 2012: 183). Within the catalogue below are Type C vervels from Angmering, West Sussex (**Ci10**) and Thwaite, Suffolk (**Cii04**) which display the Royal Stuart arms, reinforced by inscriptions of the names of *Kyng James* and *King Charlles* (respectively), and also a vervel from Cley next the Sea, Norfolk (**Ci05**) with the badge of the Prince of Wales and the inscription *Henrye Prince*.

The Bedford Estate's well-preserved and researched records are a fruitful source of information about the pursuit of falconry by the Russells in the 17th century. Two member of the family, William Russell (1616-1700), the 5th Earl and 1st Duke, and his son, William Lord Russell (1639-83), are associated with vervels in the catalogue below (**A10** and **A11**, respectively), and the estate records document how much the Earl (in particular) invested in the sport. Vervels are listed amongst other falconry equipment (including swivels, jesses, bells), which, combined with the birds' food (which included live pigeons), the total cost for their upkeep averaged about £30 to £40 a year in the mid-17th century. This is against at least a similar amount spent each year solely on the acquisition of new birds: in 1671 that sum was £51 (after Thompson 1940: 230).

The *Calendars of State Papers, Domestic* (CoSD) for the reigns of Elizabeth I, James I, Charles I and II also have information relating to falconry. Some of these records are fairly generalised and mundane, such as appointments of and payments to the Masters of the Kings Hawks and various falconers for the maintenance and training of the birds. Others are very specific, like the money approved for the construction of bridges over the River Lea in Hackney to enable James I to follow his hawks in Hoddesdon (CoSD, James I: vol. 6, 1604) or the command that residents of several towns in Hertfordshire were not to plough their arable land 'in narrow ridges, nor to suffer swine to go abroad unringed and root holes' lest the ground be made dangerous for the King and his son whilst hawking and hunting (CoSD, James I: vol. 93, 1617). They also contain instances where birds were given as diplomatic gifts or favours, such as the white hawks from Muscovy which 'the King is most pleased with' (CoSD, James I: vol. 94, 1617) or acquired through purchase. The papers give an idea of the scale and importance of some falconry events among the elite, such as in the detail of the expenses incurred (£25 to £30 a day) in hosting a French falconer and his 16 casts (pairs) of hawks, who had come to London as part of Twelfth Night celebrations and was kept on to instruct locals in falconry (CoSD, James I: vol. 158, 1624). The *State Papers* also convey something of the frequency with which the monarchs and the nobility spent their time hawking or hunting, since there are multiple examples of subjects of the Crown pursuing these activities. The *Calendar of State Papers, Scotland* (CoSS) reinforces that impression, specifically with respect to Mary, Queen of Scots (r.1542-67), who (during the early years of her captivity in England) appealed for the freedom to be allowed to ride out to hawk and hunt (CoSS: vol. 3, 1569-71). Overall the *State Papers* give a clear indication of the scale of falconry and its widespread popularity among the upper classes in the 16th and 17th centuries, and given the frequency with which it was engaged in. Therefore, the loss of material culture associated with the sport is understandable, and to be expected.

There is no specific mention of vervels in the State Papers, but they do appear in the contemporaneous *Calendar of the Cecil Papers in Hatfield House* (CCP). On a date around 20 August 1604, Sir John Roper (d.1618) wrote to Lord Cecil (1563-1612), to arrange a time for one of Roper's falconers to fly a bird for Cecil. Here it is said by Sir John '[The falconer] desires to have *a vervel of you to be put on [the bird] before he be loosed*, lest by much company and by losing him in a strange place he may rake out flying full of spirit' (CCP: August 1604, 11-20). This suggests that vervels may not have been employed in every flight, and whether to equip a bird with one (or a pair) may have been down to the judgement of the falconer, depending on the nature of the outing and the relative risk of the bird going astray. This is reinforced by a letter from the Earl of Lincoln (1539-1616) to Cecil on 10 February 1601 where he states that 'I have found the best gerfalcon for the herne in England, which I had lost.... I will enter her once again, and then present her to you for such a hawk as you never had. I pray you send me your varvel, for that I intend to fly her about London and fear that a herne should carry her so far as I may be in danger to lose her again' (sic) (CCP: February 1601, 1-10). Again, there is the hint that the person doing the flying is making a judgement that vervels are warranted for a particular occasion, and maybe the sport of catching (but not killing) herons popular with the aristocracy at this time was seen as particularly risky, especially as more than one bird of prey was utilised in such 'hunts' (van Gerven, *pers. comm.*). Additionally, it is clear that just because the bird may sport an individual's vervel, that person may not be present at the occasion a bird is flown.

This also begs questions about the ownership of birds of prey at any given time. The Cecil Papers demonstrate the usefulness of the sport in strengthening social and political bonds, and keeping in the favour of important persons. It seems that some birds were acquired and trained with the express purpose of thereafter gifting them. A series of gentlemen including the aforementioned Sir John Roper and Sir Richard Gifford (1577-1643; Lord of the manor in King's Somborne, close to the findspot of **A10**) wrote to Cecil on several occasions (cf. 7 August, 1 October, CCP: vol. 17, 1605) to apologise for their inability to present him with birds which they had been training for some time with the intention of giving to him, but who fail to live up to their expectations. Such is these gentlemen's wish to please Lord Cecil that they send him substitute birds instead, along with freshly killed quarry, to demonstrate their prowess. In the case of Sir Arthur Chichester (1563-1613), he sends 'a goshawk, a tarcell, a falcon and a cast of tarsell gentles' to Lord Cecil, saying his 'purpose was to have presented you [Lord Cecil] with more...' (July 19, CCP: Vol. 18, 1606).

Art Historical Sources

Representations of birds of prey in art have a long history. During the Anglo-Saxon period raptors were admired for their hunting skills and are commonly found on material culture of the period, including on dress accessories and in illuminated manuscripts (Webster 2012: 25 & 35 etc; Lewis & Speakman 2016: 43-4). By the end of the early medieval period (at least) it is apparent that hawks and kestrels were kept by the social elite and used for hunting. For example, in the Bayeux Tapestry (c.1072-7) they are shown being used on the hunt and also to identify men of status, including Duke William of Normandy and Harold Godwinson. Hawks are valued in the Domesday Book at the large sum of £10, and it is known Earl Harold once owned a 'hunting book', now lost (Lewis 2007: 114). Likewise, in a calendar illustration for October, dated to the middle of the 11th century (British Library, Cotton Tiberius B.v, fol.7), two men are showing hawking various birds, including ducks.

By the High Middle Ages representations of birds of prey in art become increasingly common. Not only are they associated with the nobility, but also courtly romance. In the British Museum is an ivory plaque (1878,1101.40; Fig. 3), dated to 1300-50, that shows a couple riding on a hunt together – notably it is the woman who holds

Fig. 3: Couple hunting with a hawk on an ivory plaque in the British Museum (© The Trustees of the British Museum).

Fig. 4: South Netherlandish wool tapestry of a hawking party (courtesy of the Metropolitan Museum of Art).

the hawk (Lewis & Speakman 2016: 170-1). Also in its collection is a 13th-century seal matrix (1920,0415.8) belonging to Matilda de Scalers (ibid. 169). Two women are shown hunting cranes with hawks in the *Queen Mary Psalter* (British Library, Royal 2, B.vii, fol.178) of c.1310-20, and of similar date is a queen with a small hunting bird in the *De Lisle Psalter* (British Library, Arundel 83, fol. 127). The Metropolitan Museum of Art has a 'South Netherlandish' wool tapestry (41.100.195; Fig. 4) of c.1500-1530, depicting a four-person hawking party, consisting of a man and woman astride one horse and in front of them a woman riding side-saddle on another, with a man standing in front of her. The foremost woman holds a bird of prey in her gauntleted left hand. Another famous representation is the woman with a small bird (which has been interpreted as a kestrel, but looks more like a parakeet) in the Unicorn Tapestry of c.1500, now in the Cluny Museum, Paris (CI.10831); the scene probably representing 'taste'.

These depictions of medieval women engaged in falconry are particularly interesting, not least because all the vervels recorded here – both from the Middle Ages and later (see catalogue below) – only seem to name male owners of the birds. Perhaps this reflects a significant social change regarding hawking moving into the late 16th and early 17th centuries.

An interesting depiction of hawking is that shown in an Italian manuscript illumination of the second third of the 13th century (Biblioteca Apostolica Vaticana, MS Pal. Lat. 1071, f.69), where a falconer comes to the aid of his bird. Here the hawk has been distracted by its prey on the other side of a lake (Oggins 2004: 19), so then (as now) birds were easily lost.

Compared to the overall amount of depictions of birds of prey from the late medieval to the post-medieval period, those showing vervels (as might be expected) are few. This is probably due to their small size making them difficult or unimportant to illustrate. This is apparent in a well-known Hans Holbein portrait of Robert Cheseman (1485-1547) from 1533, now in the Mauritshuis, Den Hague, where the jesses are wound through Cheseman's fingers and disappear below the frame of the picture, with one end curling up and reappearing to the left of his middle finger; here it is impossible to tell if the jess terminates in a knot or a tiny vervel. Likewise, Titian's (Tiziano Vecellio) painting of *Giorgio Cornaro with a Falcon*, of 1537, and now in the Joslyn Art Gallery, Omaha (1942.3), shows the subject holding the bird aloft on his left hand, again with the jesses wrapped through his fingers. Here they appear to end in leather buttons (where the jess has been folded over on itself), but, intriguingly, between Cornaro's third and fourth fingers protrude two shiny lozenge shaped items, and below his little finger is another small object that may be attached to the jesses. Perhaps these are meant to represent vervels, although the detail is too obscure to be sure.

There are, however, some illustrations where vervels are quite clearly shown. Compiled for the Holy Roman Emperor, Rudolf II of Habsburg (1552-1612), between 1590 and 1610, the second part of a *Bestiary* in the Austrian National Library (Cod. Min 129-30) contains a drawing of a magnificent white gyrfalcon. Here appears two vervels, of which one is shown as a ring with horizontal shield (Type Cii); this, apparently, shows a two-headed eagle, corresponding to the arms of the Holy Roman Empire (Morel & Horobin 2018: 23).

Vervels also appear in late medieval tapestries, including some already mentioned. Dating from 1430-50, and probably made in Arras, France, the *Devonshire Hunting Tapestries,* in the Victoria & Albert Museum, London (specifically the *Falconry Tapestry*; Fig. 5) show several birds with what are either Type A (washer) or Type B (ring) vervels, one on each jess, while the animals are in flight, and also grounded. In the same series, in the *Deer Hunt Tapestry*, hawks are being flown, in pairs, to attack a heron. In both *La chasse du faucon* tapestry, of about 1450, in the Musée des Arts Décoratifs, Château de Saumur, and the aforementioned Unicorn Tapestries (but the sixth in the series – À Mon Seul Désir; Cl. 10834), of about 1500, in the Musée de Cluny, there are shown hawks, both with

pairs of Type A (washer) vervels trailing from their jesses behind (Vincent 1994: 79-81). Similar is found in painted art, such as in the Flemish oil-painting by David Teniers the Younger (1610-90), *Heron Hunting with the Archduke Leopold-Guillaume*, in the Louvre.

More than a century later, the frontspiece to the 1614 edition of *Latham's Falconry* displays a hawk on its perch encircled by the tools of the falconer's trade (not depicted to scale; Fig. 6). Here, clearly visible among these items (and next to a bell) is an item that can only reasonably be understood as a vervel, being distinctly of the Type Ci (ring with shield attached vertically) variety. A plain (apparently flat) ring below it might be interpreted as a Type A (washer), or possibly Type B (ring), vervel, though Latham's drawing does not feature any inscription. Similarly, the front-piece to Edmund Bert's (1619) *An Approved Treatise of Hawkes and Hawking* features a perched bird surrounded by falconry items, again including a bell and a probable Type B (ring) vervel (Fig. 7). As noted above, *L'Encyclopédie* by Denis Diderot and Jean le Rond d' Alembert (1751-72) clearly illustrates an inscribed Type A vervel, identified as belonging to the French king.

The function of acting as a point of attachment for a leash could be performed equally by a simple ring as opposed to a vervel, or even better by a swivel. Swivels are the items preferred by modern falconers to prevent the jesses from twisting around each other (Leigh Holmes, *pers. comm.*),

Fig. 5: Detail from the Falconry Tapestry, Devonshire Hunting Tapestries in the Victoria & Albert Museum (© The Victoria and Albert Museum).

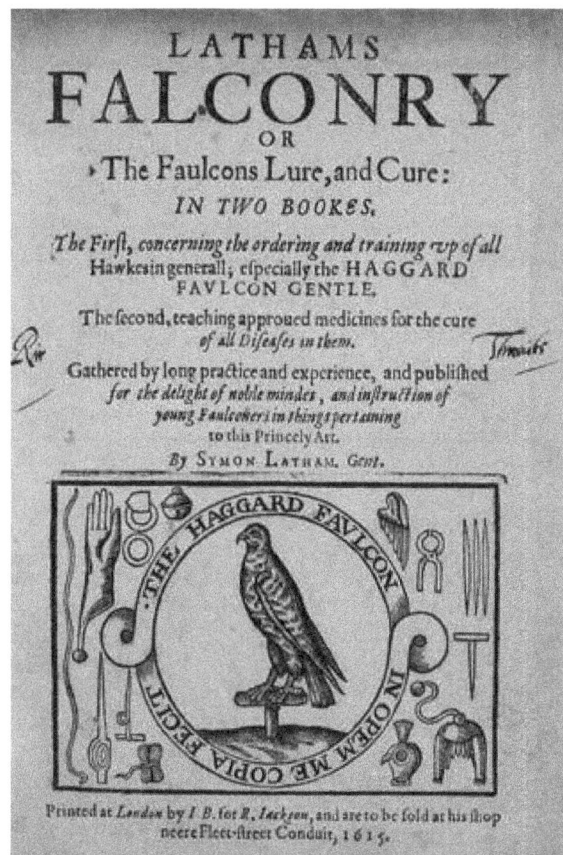

Fig. 6: Front-piece to *Latham's Falconry*.

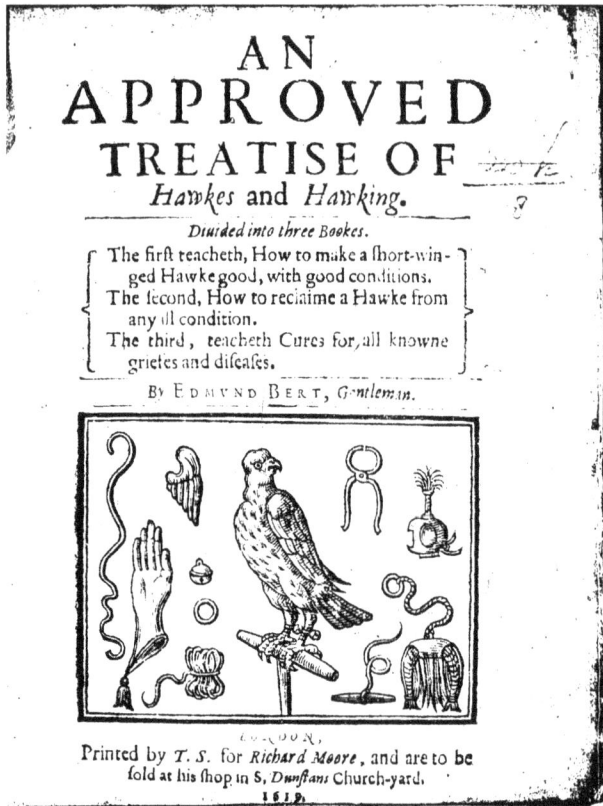

Fig. 7: Front-piece to *An Approved Treatise on Hawkes and Hawking.*

which, it has been argued were introduced by 'foreigners' (seemingly the Dutch), along with 'longer jesses', which (apparently) lessened the weight birds had to carry and also limited the chances of hawks becoming entangled in trees and other vegetation (see Morel & Horobin 2018: 28). A number of swivels have been recorded by the Portable Antiquities Scheme in recent years (see for example, NLM-B272AD), and by the mid-19th century books, such as the *Traité de Fauconnerie* (Schlegel & Wulverhorst 1853), have illustrations of birds tethered with uninscribed rings and swivels.

Antiquarian Finds

Until recently, little had been previously written about inscribed vervels, simply because few had been found and recorded. In England and Wales this situation has changed, thanks primarily to the Treasure Act 1996 – which requires the reporting of all gold and silver objects over 300 years old, amongst other items – and the work of the Portable Antiquities Scheme – established to encourage the recording of archaeological finds found by the public. Now almost 100 vervels have been found and recorded, all discovered by metal-detector users and all listed in the catalogue below.

In essence, prior to the commencement of the Treasure Act, in September 1997, there were few published examples of historic vervels and those that were published, or were in public collections, often had incomplete information regarding their provenance.

Writing as late as 1984, archaeologist Richard Ivens (1984: 132) could only cite two known examples of 'hawk rings'. One was from Hedingham Castle, inscribed 'Ox – en – for – de', and another published in the *Gentleman's Magazine* of June 1795, inscribed '*Sum regis Anglie*' (on one side) and '*Et comitis Herefordie* (sic)' on the other, which was shown by Henry Miles to the Society of Antiquaries of London. The second, and aforementioned, example was acquired by the British Museum (1855,1201.217) in a sale of the collection of Ralph Bernal, although the cataloguer knew not its function, describing it as 'a very small round gold circle like the rim of a brooch' (Christie et al 1855: 280); this despite the fact that the *Gentleman's Magazine* (1795: 474),which included a drawing of both sides of the vervel, had accurately described it as a 'hawk ring' and records it having been found near Biggleswade, Bedfordshire.

These two vervels were also quoted in the Society of Antiquaries report of 1869 when a Mr Dillon exhibited six other silver vervels. These hawking rings eventually found their way into the collection of the Victoria & Albert Museum (see appendix). Unfortunately Mr Dillon does not report the earlier provenance of the items, and it is possible that they had never entered the archaeological record, instead being passed down from their original 17th century owners.

The British Museum has another eight vervels in its collection (see Appendix B); one of these is featured in this catalogue (**Cii04**) and was acquired through the Treasure Act, and has a known findspot, but the remaining seven have come through antiquarian collectors and so there is no firm archaeological provenance for them. It is possible that Ivens (1984) was aware of these vervels but declined to mention them because they lacked provenance.

At least one further vervel was in a British public collection at the time of Ivens work, and that is a vervel with the inscription '*Garboldishm ^ Norff*', found in Harling, Norfolk, and acquired by Norwich Castle Museum (1978:422). Here it is important to note that archaeologists working for Norfolk County Council began liaising with members of the public who were discovering archaeological material prior to the implementation of the Treasure Act and the establishment of the Portable Antiquities Scheme. As a result of this work four further vervels discovered before 1997 were published in *Norfolk Archaeology* (Ashley & Rogerson 1997; Margeson 1994; Gaimster & Margeson 1989) and acquired by Norwich Castle Museum (see Appendix B).

The vervels from Norfolk are the only examples from the archaeological record of England and Wales found prior to 1997 where precise findspots are known. More surprising perhaps is that no vervels have been found in Scotland, especially since Scottish law – the Common Law of Treasure Trove – requires all archaeological finds to be reported (this will be discussed further below). As has already been noted, falconry was practiced in Scotland, just as it was further south, and there are numerous references to the activity in the *Calendar of State Papers, Scotland* (CoSS) in the time of the reign of Elizabeth I.[2] Stuart Campbell (*pers. comm.*), formerly of the Scottish Treasure Trove Unit, believes that the lack of vervels found and reported by metal-detectorists in Scotland may demonstrate a relative scarcity in the archaeological record, since most detectorists will, through information available on the internet, be able to recognise a vervel if they find one. If that is the case, it probably illustrates a significant difference in the scale to which falconry was practiced in Scotland as compared to England in the period before 1700. Indeed, it is the case that only two vervels have been found in the last 20 years from Wales, and none from Northern Ireland.

Classification

There are broadly four types of vervels (A to D) of which Type C can be divided into three subtypes (i to iii).

Simplest in construction are those that are of 'washer form' (**Type A**; Fig. 8), a flat circular ring that is sub-rectangular in section; it is likely the edges were smoothed when such items were produced, then exacerbated by wear. These are normally inscribed on both sides (see catalogue) but not always. These are the commonest vervel type, with 35 examples being recorded.

Several vervels appear similar in form to banded finger-rings (**Type B**; Fig. 9). These are circular in plan, and sub-rectangular or D-shaped in section. As with Type A vervels the edges of the ring can be rounded, probably intentionally to save damage to the leather jesses of the bird or its leash. The inscription on these is always on the outside of the band. 22 examples of this vervel type have been reported and recorded over the last 20 years.

Diagnostic of **Type C** vervels is a 'shield attached' to the loop or ring. As indicated above, this occurs in three different ways. All together 26 have been found and recorded, so these are the most common type after Type A vervels.

First (**Type Ci**; Fig. 10), the shield-shaped plate might be soldered to the ring vertically; in essence the ring is no different to that on Type B vervels. These are commonest of the Type C vervels, with 13 known examples.

Similar are those with a shield-shaped plate soldered horizontally (**Type Cii**; Fig. 11). As with Type Ci vervels, the ring is circular in plan and normally of D-shape section. It is usually the case that the shield is joined to the ring where the ring is joined also. Seven of these have been recorded.

The final Type C vervel (**Type Ciii**; Fig. 12) takes the form of a shield-shaped plate above which is an integrally cast ring (so the ring and shield are not soldered together). The ring or hoop can vary in size. In many cases these will have an engraved design, such as a heraldic crest, rather than lettering, though it might be the case there is some

Fig. 8: Type A vervel (A33 in this catalogue) (courtesy of the Portable Antiquities Scheme).

Fig. 9: Type B vervel (B01 in this catalogue) (courtesy of the Portable Antiquities Scheme).

Fig. 10: Type Ci vervel (Ci02 in this catalogue) (courtesy of the Portable Antiquities Scheme).

Fig. 11: Type Cii vervel (Cii01 in this catalogue) (courtesy of the Portable Antiquities Scheme).

---

[2] Several of these references are in communiqués from ambassador Thomas Randolph to William Cecil: 1 April 1563 'Since the beginning of the Queen's sorrows, she has taken pleasure to ride up and down, hawking and hunting daily from place to place'; 12 November 1864 'Murray and Lethington have leave to ride into the Merse hawking' (CoSS: vol. 2, 1563-9).

Fig. 12: Type Ciii vervel (Ciii04 in this catalogue) (courtesy of the Portable Antiquities Scheme).

lettering within the design. In total six examples of this sub-type have been recorded and reported over the last 20 years.

Some variations on these types can be expected, as falconers experimented to find the most useful equipment. As has been noted above, Sir Thomas Sherley (1603) describes an invention of his, a 'garter' form vervel, that went directly around the leg of a hunting bird and thus (he claimed) was much less likely to be lost than the traditional vervel. The British Museum has what appears to be a garter in its collection (1913,0710.8), and a single, though incomplete, example (**D01**) has been reported as Treasure via the Portable Antiquities Scheme. Here this type is listed as **Type D**, formed of two silver strips, rectangular in section and semi-circular in plan, which are then hinged together. These vervels, as might be expected, are only inscribed on their exterior face.

For decorated rings that lack an inscription (see Appendix A – potential vervels), it is their small diameter (assumed to be too narrow to be worn as a finger-ring) which has led the recorders of these objects to assume that they are hawking rings. While they may have served as links for the leathers of hunting birds, or had another function, their lack of inscription means they would not have been useful in assisting the return of lost hunting birds.

It is intriguing that some authorities (mostly on the continent) occasionally classify heraldic harness pendants as vervels, for example at the Falconry and Cigar-Makers Museum in Valkenswaard, Netherlands, which has a selection on display. Likewise, the examples illustrated by Th. Vincent in his 1994 article on vervels appear to show just harness pendants. While the documentary sources he cites for the manufacture of vervels for various members of the French nobility in the later medieval period do suggest that some vervels were enamelled, as harness pendants are, they also tended to be for articles of silver, engraved with the name of the owner. This includes, for example, the order by Philip the Good (1396-1467) for:

'24 douzaines de vervelles d'argent doré, dont la moitié taillez et esmaillliez des armes de Philippe le Bon,

Fig. 13: Type D vervel (D01 in this catalogue) (courtesy of the Portable Antiquities Scheme).

l'autre moitié aussi esmailliez et escript a l'entour de chacune "duc de Bourgogne et de Brabant"' (24 dozen silver-gilt vervels, engraved with the arms of Philip the Good on one face, and the other face engraved with the script "Duke of Burgundy and the Brabant") (ibid: 78).

So, it is not entirely clear why he, and others, are confident that uninscribed base-metal enamelled pendants, often much heavier than the vervels catalogued here (ibid: illustration I), are themselves vervels. In England, these items, which are very common metal-detector finds (more than 5,000 of medieval date have been recovered), are always identified with horse riding gear (Griffiths 1986).

There is, however, an object described as a 'falkenmarke' in the Kunsthistorisches Museum, Vienna (D50), which looks very much like a harness pendant, and is about the same size and weight, but has a clear ring, like that on Type Cii vervels. It is also enamelled with the arms of an individual (Anne de Montmorency), which is less common on vervels, but typical of harness pendants. It is significant that none of these harness-pendant like 'vervels' have been found in England, or at least they have not been identified as such.

Construction

Although some earlier sources (see for example Diderot & D'Alembert 1751-72) discuss vervels being made of copper-alloy, the archaeological evidence points to most being made of precious metal, normally silver. As noted above, only one example in this catalogue (**A03**) has been identified as being made of a non-precious metal, though since the metallurgy of the object (like most in this catalogue) was not tested there is a possibility that it was produced of highly debased silver; indeed, this vervel from Burcott, Buckinghamshire is somewhat significant since it belonged to a hawk of Andrew Pitcairn (d.1642), Chief Falconer to King Charles I (r.1625-49) from 1626.

The metallic composition of only a few vervels has been tested. From Thwaite, Suffolk (**Cii04**) the hawking ring associated with a King Charles (I or II) was tested by the British Museum and found to be of 97% silver. Similar was the composition of a vervel from Bronington, Wrexham (**A35**) of unclear ownership association, which was analysed by the National Museums Wales using a scanning electron microscope (SEM), plus energy dispersive X-ray spectrometer (EDX), indicating it to

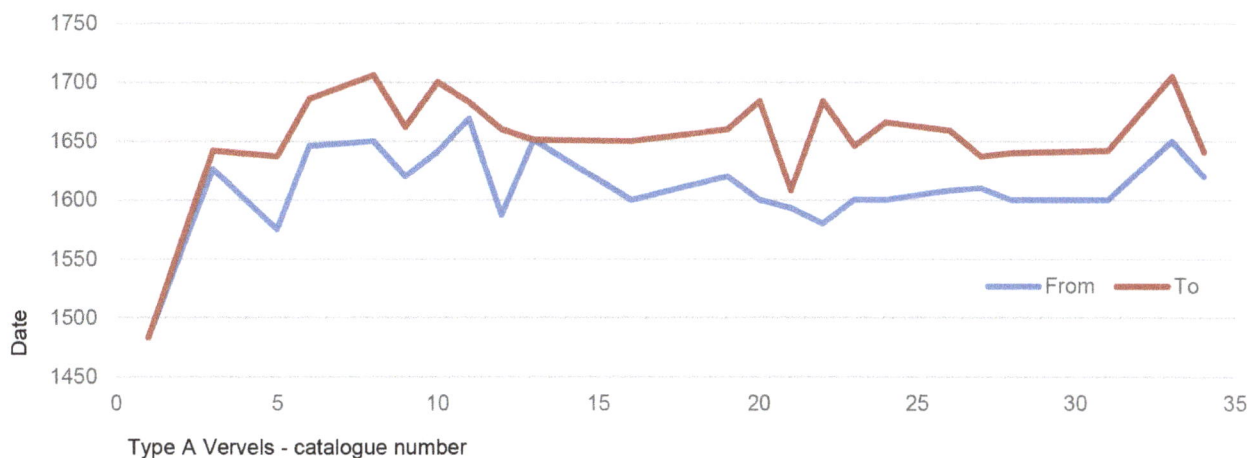

Graph 1: Type A vervels – by date.

be approximately 96% silver and 4% copper. Of lesser quality silver was a vervel from Stourport-on-Severn, Worcestershire (**Ci13**), linked to the Eyton family, that was tested by Birmingham Museums Trust (twice) on the surface of the shield, and found to have a metallic content of 93.88-93.24% silver, 2.9-2.48% copper, 3.7-3.44% iron and 0.2-15% lead. The ring was also tested and found to be 86.55% silver, 0.93% copper, 10.57% iron, 0.29% tin, 0.13% lead, and 0.76% bromine. Given vervels were not mass produced, variation in their composition is to be expected, though it is of note that those which have been tested (albeit a small percentage of the total) are relatively pure.

As part of the work for this publication, the remainder of the British Museum's collection of silver vervels has been scientifically tested. This revealed that these seven vervels had a silver content of between c.82% to c.95%, with percentages of copper that vary from c.4.1% to c.16.2%. Two of the vervels, both under the reference number 1927,0216.68 (one inscribed *Will Lord Sherard* and the other *Will Sherard of*) are very similar in metallic composition, as would be expected.

Gold vervels are also known, but are excessively rare, and none have been found in the last 20 years. The aforementioned example from the British Museum's collection (1855,1201.217) found near Biggleswade, Bedfordshire was associated with Henry IV (r.1399-1413), and is inscribed (in Latin) 'I belong to the King of England'. It seems likely, as the inscription on this item suggests, that gold was only used on elite vervels, although silver vervels in this catalogue show lesser precious metals were also favoured for royal hawking rings (see **A01**). The softness of gold might suggest it was not as practical as silver, though this does depend on how the vervel was used (see below). The British Museum vervel was also analysed and found to contain 96% gold, 2.3% silver and 1.6% copper.

None of the vervels recorded here (or in the museum collections listed in Appendix B) bear a maker's mark (save perhaps **B15**) or any means of identifying the goldsmith

who made them. That might be expected, given their tiny proportions.[3] Even so, many small 16th-17th century items – such as finger-rings, buttons and thimbles – bear such marks, and Type C vervels (in particular) would appear to have enough space to allow for a maker's mark to be stamped. This perhaps suggested they were made in local workshops, and it mattered little that their precious metal content was pure – though we can see from vervels that have been scientifically tested, that they were made of good metals.

Dating

An approximate date for most of the vervels reported as Treasure via the Portable Antiquities Scheme is to the 17th century. Some hawking rings can be identified with historical characters which obviously aid their dating accuracy, but for most their dating is predominantly based on the form and style of their inscriptions. The earliest vervel recorded in the catalogue below appears to be of about 1483 (**A01**). Others are quite securely dated in the 16th century, or into the late 18th century.

In the case of Type A vervels that can be dated with a relative degree of accuracy, so excluding those dated to a whole century, and also **A01** and **A14** (both of medieval date), the earliest *from* date is 1575 with the latest *to* date being 1706 (Graph 1). This gives a mean average of 1610-54 for those that can be closely dated. If those with a century or half century *from* or *to* date are excluded (i.e. those that have the most approximate dates), this gives a refined average of 1609-52.

In the case of Type B vervels that can be dated with some certainty, the earliest *from* date is c.1550, and the latest *to* date is 1786 (Graph 2). This gives a mean average of 1604-63 for those that can be dated with relative accuracy, and a refined average (as explained above) of 1619-64.

---

[3]   However, the first official exemption for 'silver wire and articles which by reason of their smallness were incapable of being stamped with the prescribed marks' from the need to be assayed was in an Act of 1696 under William III (Jackson 1921: 18).

Inscribed Vervels

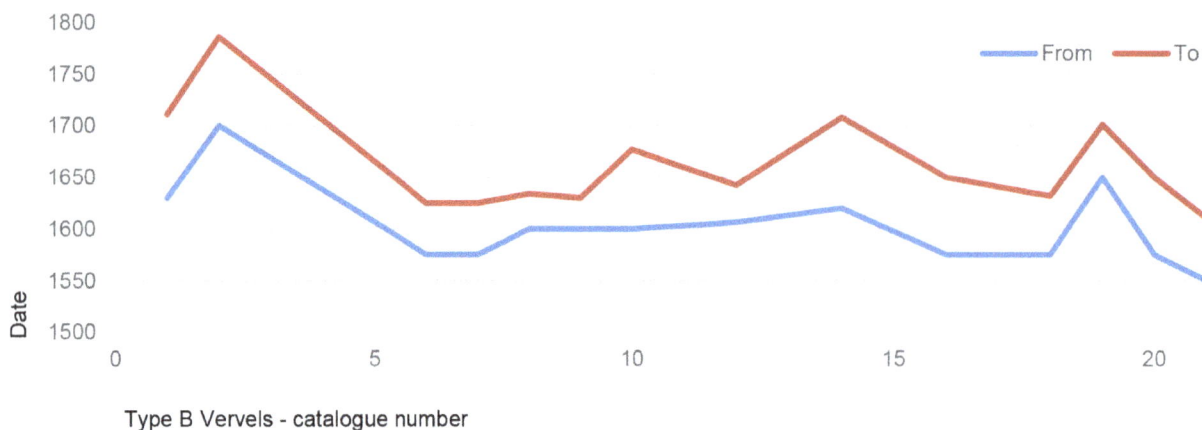

Graph 2: Type B vervels – by date.

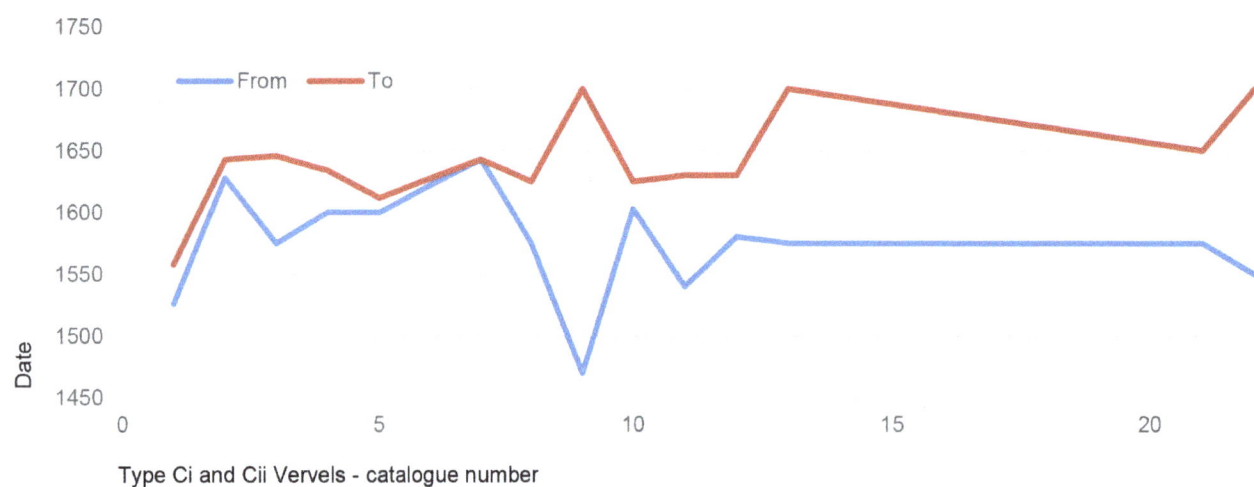

Graph 3: Type Ci and Cii vervels – by date.

Type Ci and Type Cii vervels are considered here together because of their similarity (Graph 3). Many can be dated with some certainty, though within this group are several that are dated to centuries or half-centuries, which is particularly the case for Type Cii vervels. The earliest *from* date is 1526, and the latest *to* date is 1700. This gives a mean average of 1573-1643 for those that can be dated with relative accuracy, and a refined average of 1577-1637.

There are only a small number of Type Ciii vervels (six), but the date of these is worth considering independently of the other Type C vervels because they significantly differ in both size and weight (see below) (Graph 4). The earliest *from* date for these is c.1500, and the latest *to* date is c.1650, therefore giving a mean average of 1529-88, and a refined average of 1536-92.

The ability to date vervels allows them to be understood chronologically for the first time (Graph 5). On the basis of the vervels reported as Treasure via the Portable Antiquities Scheme, it seems that Type Ciii vervels are the earliest type, coming into common use in the second quarter of the 16th century and then going out of fashion later that century. Next are the closely related Type Ci and Cii vervels, which are common from the last quarter of the

16th century, then falling out of use by the second quarter of the 17th century.

Hardest to makes sense of are Type A vervels. Whilst those discovered in recent years seems to suggest they became common from the beginning of the 17th century until about the 1650s, it is apparent (on the basis of art-historical and archaeological evidence) that they date back at least to the late Middle Ages, even as far back as the 12th century perhaps. They also have longevity, well in to the later 17th century, confirmed also by art depictions.

Similar are Type B vervels, which appear to have been in concurrent use with Type A vervels, though (perhaps) coming into popular use a bit later, and probably outliving them; the later Type B vervels are in use some 80 years after those of Type A.

The only Type D vervel in the catalogue below is of broad 17th century date, which makes some sense if Sir Thomas Sherley really did invent this type in 1603. Their popularity seems limited.

On this basis, and as might be expected, heraldic arms/ badges on vervels were gradually phased out in favour

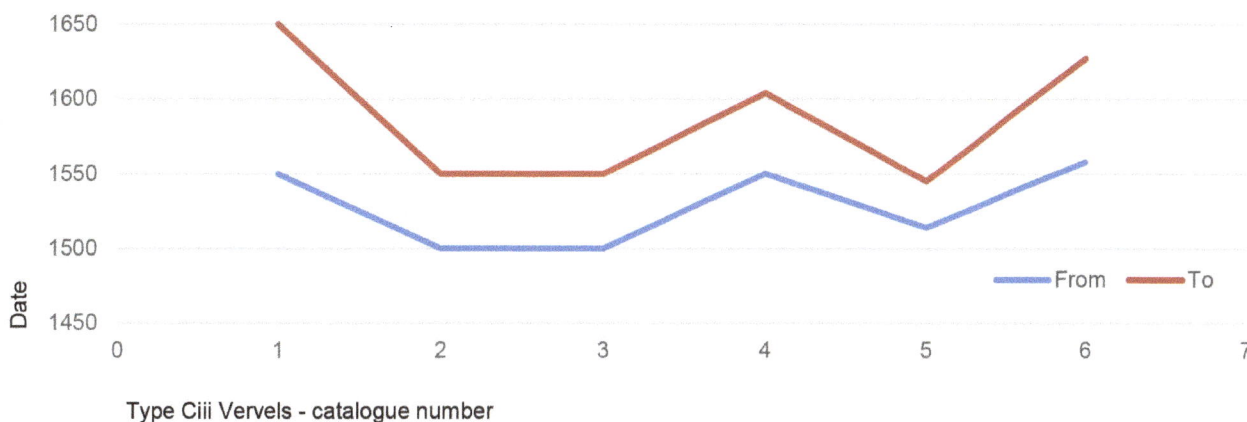

Graph 4: Type Ciii vervels – by date.

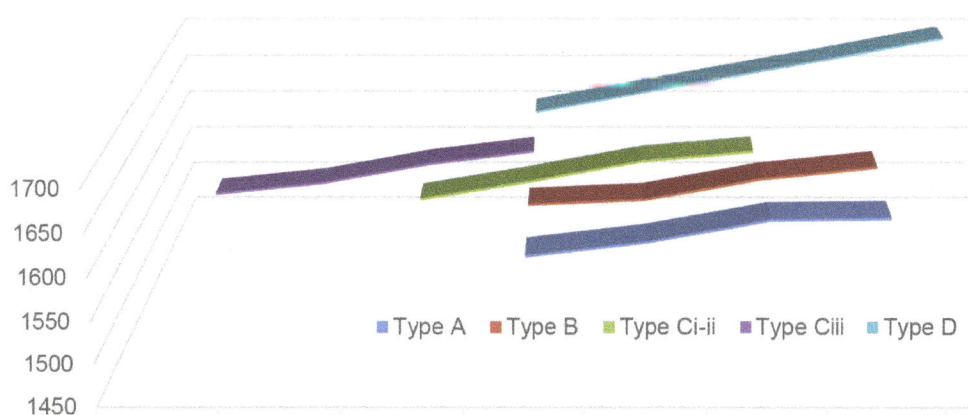

Graph 5: Vervel types – chronology.

of those with text-based inscriptions. This is likely to coincide with a general decline in the population at large to interpret heraldic arms (perhaps as they became more sophisticated), and the fact that more people were able to read and write. Furthermore, perhaps simple rings and washers were more practical (less burdensome) and less prone to tangling a bird whilst it was being flown.

Inscriptions

Without an inscription (or inscribed motif) it is impossible to know whether a vervel is actually a vervel at all; at the end of the catalogue below there is a list of possible uninscribed vervels (Appendix A), although these objects might have served other purposes. Inscriptions upon hawking rings may be decorative and/or written, and there is a high degree of variation in these elements, which is typical of individually constructed (man-made, non-mass-produced) objects.

Although the function of inscriptions upon hawking rings might seem obvious, it is probably incorrect to assume that they all served only to identify the ownership of hunting birds lost in the wild. While the inscriptions upon some vervels make it clear they were devices to enable the return of lost birds – as with the aforementioned **B18**, which has upon it 'RETORNE TO

HVGH PORTMAN', and **A06**, inscribed with 'Returne to Gilbert Hodey' – in most other instances the message on the vervel is less prescriptive, perhaps just marking the bird's ownership and not stating how this information should be used. It is highly likely, for example, that some vervels might be used to identify the ownership of hawks when kept with those belonging to other individuals, such as those in communal lodging at a stately home, or birds taken out together as part of a hunting party, such as in a cadge, as illustrated in *L'Encyclopédie* (Diderot & D'Alembert 1751-72: pl.8). Such instances might be inferred by places in the landscape where several vervels, naming a variety of individuals, have been found – as at Micheldever, Hampshire, where vervels naming William Russell (**A11**), Henry Browne (**B06**) and William Wollascott (**A12**) were all recovered, and which will be further discussed in due course.

As has already been mentioned, some vervels are decorated with a design, normally a coat of arms, aspects thereof (such as a badge or crest), or other heraldic inspired motif. Because of their form, these designs lend themselves to vervels with shields (Type C). Full arms are found on a number of hawking rings, including that of Charles Brandon (**Ciii05**) and John St John of Bletsoe (**Ci01**), as well as the Royal Arms (**Ci10**, **Cii04** and **Ciii04**). Unsurprisingly, given the small size of hawking rings, more common are heraldic badges and crests – serving as abbreviations for full heraldic arms; particularly in Types Ci and Cii. Noteworthy is a vervel which has upon its shield the image of a bird with outstretched wings on a gloved hand, marking the ownership of Robert Dormer, the Earl of Carnarvon (**Ci02**), and the badge of the Prince of Wales, on a vervel denoting Henry Frederick (**Ci05**), the eldest son of James I and Anne of Denmark. It is often the case, not least because many vervels are found without their coloured enamelling, that an inscription is also needed to make sense of the heraldry. Take for example a hawking ring associated with Edward Hunne (**Ci06**), which shows the common heraldic device of a lion rampant, which has now lost its colour.

By the 17th century, when vervels become particularly common, and heraldry had become extremely complex (because of the increased granting of arms and intermarriage between the nobility, especially where the incorporation of the arms of preeminent pedigrees were desired), it is unlikely that most everyday people would have been able to identify the ownership of most lost hawks based on the heraldry of their vervels alone. The point is made by the design of two vervels (**Ciii02 & Ciii03**) which have upon them a lion rampant, as seen on the arms of the Dukes of Norfolk, with the useful inscription T NORFOCK. Both the FitzAlans of Mowbray and Mowbrays themselves used this device, but with differing tincture. Therefore, it would have been the vervel's written inscription, as well as the geographical location of the find, that would have identified the hawk's owner – as is the case with inscribed vervels found nowadays.

Less ostentatious decorative features also occur on hawking rings, especially on Type A and B vervels. Common are stars, of five-, six-, or eight-points, as on vervels associated with William, Earl of Bedford (**A10**), William Wollascott (**A12**) and Thomas Crispe of Goudhurst (**A16**). Rarely are vervels found that have stars where their points vary in number, though examples are of that associated with the place of Melsonby, North Yorkshire (**A32**) which appears to have both six- and eight-pointed stars, and that of Shelford, probably in Suffolk (**B20**), which has both five- and six-pointed stars; it is intriguing that both these seem to name places and not individuals.

Crosses are also a popular motif on Type A and B, and some Type C, vervels. Mostly these are of simple form, as on hawking rings from Little Missenden (**A04**), Wingham (**A15**) and Hadleigh (**B16**), and those identifying Henry Clare of Stanfield Hall (**A21**). In some instances the crosses are miniscule as with a vervel from Billesley (**A27**) and may almost be mistaken for another form of punctuation. Crosses of simple form are accompanied by bursts of dashes, numbering three and five, on a vervel belonging to a hawk of John Bruen of Stapleford Hall (**A05**), and a cross formed of four dots appears on that identifying an otherwise anonymous esquire of Bisham (**A02**). The cross on the vervel from Puddleton (**B03**) is a 'cross potent' with terminals made up of short perpendicular lines.

A rare medieval vervel, associated with a Prince Edward, probably Edward V, has upon it sprigs of foliage (**A01**). These are also found on post-medieval vervels, such as those naming Gilbert Hody (**A06**) and Edmund Bruning (**A08**); the latter also has trefoils and crosses, both fleury and foliate. A foliate spray is found on a vervel from Broome, Norfolk (**B14**), also naming that place, and a vervel from Dalton, North Yorkshire (**A30**) has a nonsensical legend of crosses and vertical lines as well as sprigs of foliage; how this functioned for returning or identifying lost birds is unclear.

These small decorative elements often function as punctuation marks, or to fill blank space on hawking rings. Interesting in this respect is the use of dots like colons, such as on vervels identifying Thomas Salway of Throckmorton (**A13**) and Thomas Wigley of Middleton (**A25**). Sometimes three vertical dots may be used, as on a ring associated with Morton in Worcestershire (**A07**), or just a single dot, as on vervels naming William Spring (**A20**) and Edward Montagu (**A22**). Single dots are particularly common in the inscriptions on Type B vervels, such as from Layer-de-la-Haye (**B04**), and those of hawks once owned by Edmund Lucy (**B09**) and Richard Hardres (**B12**), but are also found on the Type C hawking ring associated with William Hansard (**Ci04**).

Inscriptions on vervels can be upper-case (capital letters) or lower-case (normally in italic script); the latter may include capital letters for initials as appropriate (Graph 6). Overall almost three-quarters (72%) of the hawking rings in the catalogue below have lower-case inscriptions, but this varies depending upon the type. In order of commonality of lower-case inscriptions, Type A have the most (89%), followed by Type B (64%) and Type C (47%) vervels; in the case of Type C vervels, two have initials only and four have no inscription (instead only having inscribed decoration). There is only a single example of a Type D vervel, which has a lower-case inscription.

The higher percentage of lower-case inscriptions found on Type A vervels makes sense in terms of their average date range, especially compared to Type C vervels (see above). Charles Oman (1974: 40-1) states that in the context of post-medieval finger-rings, upper-case inscriptions continued to be used until the mid-17th century, when they were superseded in popularity by lower-case, italic inscriptions. Lower-case inscriptions occasionally appeared on rings even before the middle of the century; the gold posy ring in the Ackworth Hoard (SWYOR-FDBB70) is dated to 1645/46 by the coins that it was found buried with and an example in the collection of the British Museum (1961,1202.115) is dated by its inscription to 1620, so it is not surprising that the vervel from the Baldock area, Hertfordshire (**B09**), for instance, is in italics but likely dates to the early 17th century. Mourning rings from the second half of the 17th century are useful sources against which to compare inscriptions. See for instance the similarity in script found on a mourning ring from Durham (DUR-4FC118) dated to 1680 by its inscription, and the

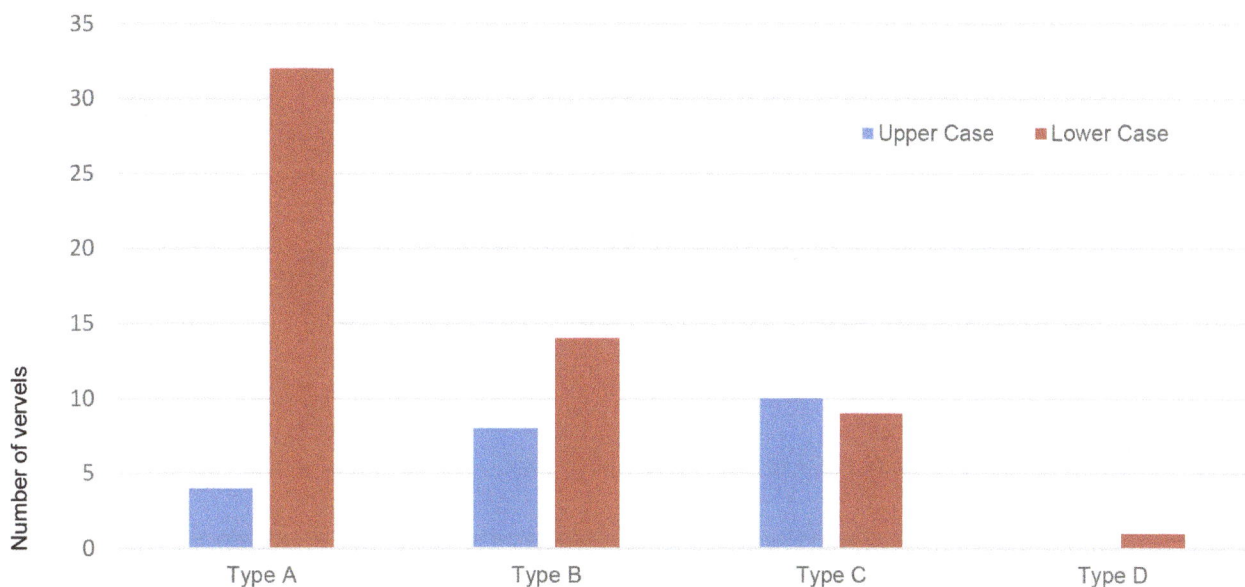

Graph 6: Inscriptions on vervels – upper-case v lower-case.

vervels from Bisham, Berkshire (**A02**) and Bronington, Wrexham (**A35**).

As might be expected, inscriptions upon vervels can be abbreviated, and names of people and places are spelt in a variety of ways.

Titles include esquire, usually abbreviated as 'Esq' (**A02**) or 'Esqr' (**A27, A34 & B12**), mister as 'Mr' (**A08**) or even 'M' (**A33**), earl as 'Earle' (**A10**) or 'Erle' (**Ci02**), and Sir as 'Sr' (**A28, B06 & B10** etc) or 'SR' (**Ci04**). Intriguingly, count ('come') appears to be written on a vervel associated with the Chester family (**A19**). 'Lord', spelt in full, is only written on one vervel in the catalogue (**A22**).

First (given/Christian) names can also be abbreviated: Edward might be 'Edw' (**A22**), Ralph as 'RAFE' (**Cii07**), Richard as 'Richa' (**B12**), Thomas could be 'Tho' (**A13 & A25**), and William might be 'WIL' (**Ci04**), 'Will' (**A09, A10 & A11**), 'WYLL' (**Cii06**) or even 'Willi*a*' (**A12**). Occasionally, extra letters will be added, as in 'Henrye' for Henry Clare/Clere (**A21**) and Henry Frederick, Prince of Wales (**Ci05**). In some inscriptions, John might be spelt with an 'I' (**A24, B05, Ci01 & Cii03**), as might be expected, and it is similar with James (**B22**).

It is not uncommon for family names to have extra letters or be spelt unconventionally, such as 'Englefeilde' for Englefield (**A09**), 'Hodey' for Hody (**A06**), 'Mountague' for Montague (**A22**) and 'Pitcairne' for Pitcairn (**A03**); these may not have been spelt consistently at the time anyway. Often family names are spelt contrary to their usual form. Lucy is written 'Luci' on Thomas Lucy's hawk's vervel (**A28**), and on Edmond Lucy's it is spelt 'Lucye' (**B09**). A vervel naming William Sheffield spells his name 'Sheffeild' (**A31**), that of John Aubrey is spelt 'Awbrey' (**A34**), and that of James Birkby as 'BERKBE' (**B22**). Robert, Earl of Carnarvon, has his name written 'Carmarvin' (**Ci02**), and a member of the Vaughan family,

perhaps Francis, as 'VAGHAN' (**Cii05**). Likewise, 'Y's replace 'i's in 'SPRYNG' for Spring (**A20**).

Places, including counties, can also be spelt variously. On a vervel of the esquire of Bisham, Berkshire is spelt 'Berckshr' (**A02**), and is 'Barcke' on a hawking ring identified with William Wollascott (**A12**). 'Buck' on a vervel of the Chester family (**A19**), appears to be for 'Buckingham'; this hawking ring also shows Chicheley as 'Chichly'. Hampshire is spelt 'Hampshrie' on a vervel from Micheldever (**B07**) – this is presumably a spelling mistake, Norfolk as 'Norff' (**B14**), 'NOR' (**B15**) or 'NOR/FOC/K' (**Ciii02 & Ciii03** – though in these cases the authors assume it is the title Duke of Norfolk being referenced), Suffolk as 'SVF' (**B16**) or 'suf' (**Ciii06**), and Wiltshire might be abbreviated as 'Wilts' (**A29**). County names might also have the prefix 'Co' as before 'Chester' on a vervel found at Bronington, Wrexham (**A35**). A vervel from Hartpury, Gloucestershire (**A07**) has Worcester spelt 'worsester', and that associated with George Ashton from Lincolnshire (**A18**) has Lincoln or Lincolnshire spelt 'lincin'.

As with personal names, towns and counties might have letters added, such as 'Buckinghame' for Buckingham (**A04**), 'Readinge' for Reading (**A12**) and 'SHELFORDE' for Shelford (**B20**). They might also be shortened, as in 'Midlton' for Middleton (**A25**), 'Bilseley' for Billesley (**A26**) and 'Wittinghã' for Whittingham (**B19**). On a vervel belonging to a hawk of the Earl of Bedford his family seat of Woburn Abbey, Bedfordshire is spelt 'Wooborne Abby' (**A10**), and one from Puddleton in Dorset has 'at mouncton in dorsett' for Monkton, Dorset (**B03**). Hadleigh in Essex is once spelt as 'HADLYGE' (**B16**) on a vervel from Wiveton, Norfolk, and Rolleston, Leicestershire, is spelled 'Roulston' on one found in Hallaton, Leicestershire (**B13**).

A vervel associated with Andrew Pitcairn (**A03**) spells 'court' (as in Royal Court) as 'Cortt'. Likewise, 'return' can be spelt with an extra 'e', as on the previously

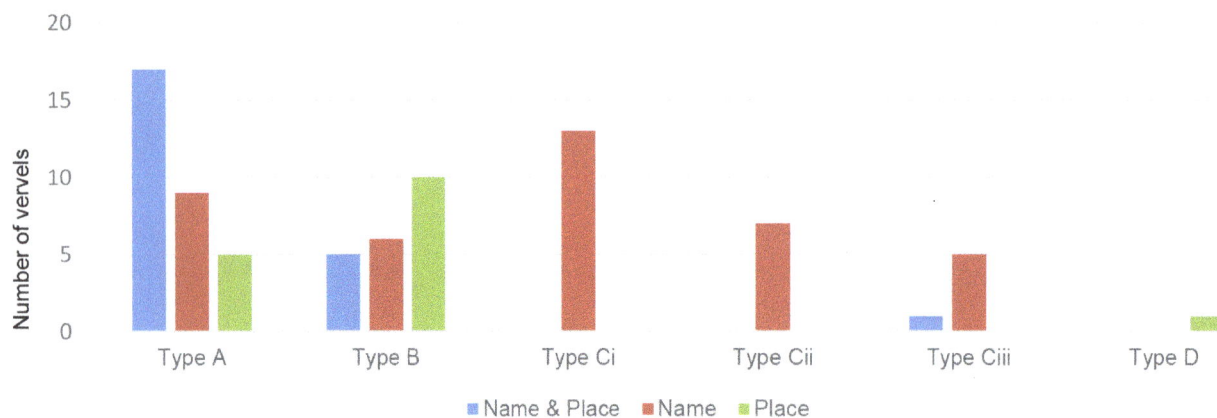

Graph 7: Inscribed vervels – and whether these name the hawk's owner and his place of residence.

mentioned vervel identified with Gilbert Hody (**A06**), and king is written 'Kyng' on a vervel associated with James I or James II (**Ci10**).

As might be expected in the 17th century, 'u's can be 'v's, as in 'GOVDHURST' on a vervel of Thomas Crispe (**A16**), in 'EDMVNTON' on another from Bucknell (**B17**), and 'HVGH' on a hawking ring (now mentioned several times) for a bird of Hugh Portman (**B18**).

It is relatively common for Type A vervels to name both the owner of the hunting bird and also the place where that individual resided, or (at least) which they owned (17 of 35 instances) (Graph 7). Take for example three Hampshire vervels, from Horndean (**A09**) which reads 'Will[iam] Englefeilde Esq of Spensers', from Kings Sombourne (**A10**) naming 'Will[iam] Earl of Bedford at Wooborne Abb[e]y', and from Micheldever (**A11**) that has upon it 'Mr Will Russell of Stratton in Hampshire'. Conversely, there are also vervels that just name the bird's owner, and not the place of their residence. Examples (nine in total) include, that from Hambledon, Hampshire (**A08**) naming 'Mr Edmund Bruning', another from Barnwell, Northamptonshire (**A22**) which has upon it 'Edw. Lord. Mountague', and one from East Chinnock, Somerset (**A24**) reading 'IOHN STRANGWAYES'. If vervels are only to identify lost birds (see discussion above) then those naming important aristocrats, like the Earl of Montague, might be more useful than those naming lesser known gentry.

The number of Type A vervels (five in total) naming just a place (and not the owners' name) is even more intriguing. Included is that from Bisham, Berkshire (**A02**) with the inscription 'Esq of Bisham…', one from Little Missenden in Buckinghamshire (**A04**) with the words 'in the County of Buckinghame', and another, from Bronington, Wrexham (**A35**), with the inscription 'Somerford Co. Chester. Esq'. Clearly these 'place name' inscriptions are not much use alone, and perhaps were worn with other identification marks – probably with another vervel naming the owners. As has already been noted, the use of two vervels being worn together are shown in both the *Devonshire Hunting* and *Unicorn* Tapestries and in some contemporary treatises. Interesting in this respect

is a vervel from Bruen Stapleford, Cheshire (**A05**), which is inscribed (on both sides of the ring) with 'J Bruen of // Stapleford in', and therefore (presumably) would have been worn with another vervel saying in 'Co Chester' or 'Cheshire' etc. Alternatively, perhaps the 'in' is an error, or the engraver ran out of room. Important in this respect is the discovery of two vervels at Minting, Lincolnshire, of which one (**A17**) reads 'George Ashton of', and the other (**A18**) has 'of Minting Lincin' – together the vervels might say 'George Ashton of // of Minting Lincoln'. Similarly, at Billesley, Warwickshire, were found two related vervels, one (**A26**) inscribed 'Sr Robert Lee // of Bilseley', and the other (**A27**) giving just his name, 'Robert Lee Esq'. These finds appear to prove that it was practice for some vervels (at least) to be used in pairs, and also (as in the case of the Minting vervels) the normality of extra words, such as (in **A18**) two uses of 'of'. Two recently discovered Type A vervels (**A14** and **A30**) have inscriptions that make little sense nowadays, and one wonders if they were more meaningful to contemporaries!

It is less common for Type B vervels to name both an individual and where they resided – indeed, only a quarter do so. In one instance the owner of a hunting bird is identified by just their initials: this example is from Horton, Dorset (**B02**) and has upon it 'HS at Horton, Dorset'. Others give full names and might have been quite useful for identifying lost birds, especially if the gentry named were well known locally. Examples include vervels associated with Sir Edmond Lucy (**B09**) and Richard Hardres (**B12**). A vervel of Sir Henry Browne found at Micheldever, Hampshire (**B06**) has the inscription 'Sr Hen. Browne of' suggesting, like some of the Type A examples above, it was worn with another ring naming the place where Sir Henry Browne lived. Similar are vervels inscribed 'Iohn Stepkin of' from near Topplesfield, Essex (**B05**) and 'Sr John Philpott of' found at Thruxton, Hampshire (**B08**). This seems to be the likely explanation for 11 vervels that only give the place of residence, including those with the inscriptions 'At mounckton in dorsett' (**B03**), 'OF. NORWOOD. IN. KENT' (**B11**) and 'HADLYGE IN SVF' (**B16**).

Type Ci vervels normally give an individual's name only (11 of 13 examples). Presumably the crest or badge on the shield associated with this vervel type further aiding identification of the hawk's owner. However, one from Spixworth, Norfolk (**Ci07**) gives only the initials of its owner on the shield – 'WC' – with the date '1643'. Another, from Lowick, Northamptonshire (**Ci09**) has the initials 'I S' and a 'Stafford knot' motif of the Stafford family, aiding the identification of the hawk's owner. Two vervels of this type only have a pictorial device, showing a wyvern (**Ci11 & Ci12**). They were both found at Collingbourne Kingston, Wiltshire, and are probably associated with local aristocrats, the Herberts, Earls of Pembroke. Also noteworthy is the inscription on a vervel from Wiveton, Norfolk (**Ci08**), with the inscription 'Tho. Gryme. of', the 'of' suggesting the vervel was used (as with some Type A and B examples above) as one of a pair.

Likewise, Type Cii vervels (also with a shield) commonly only give the name of their owner (six of seven examples). This can be abbreviated as in the vervels associated with 'F. VAGHAN' (**Cii05**), 'W / Sydnor' (**Cii01**) and 'RAFE' (**Cii07**). One, from Wereham, Norfolk (**Cii02**) only has a 'heraldic' motif, of a cross, which it has been impossible to attribute to a local individual or family.

Type Ciii vervels, also have a shield as part of their form. Two, (**Ciii01 & Ciii06**) have upon their shield the inscriptions in three and four lines, respectively, but no pictorial element. Two (**Ciii02 & Ciii03**), already discussed above, give the name and arms of the Dukes of Norfolk – 'T NORFOCK'. Another two have the Royal Arms (**Ciii04**) and the arms of Charles Brandon, Duke of Suffolk (**Ciii05**). The latter is of course significant, since it can be identified with a particular individual.

The only Type D vervel (**D01**) is incomplete, the surviving part inscribed 'Halland in Sussex'. Presumably the other half gave the name of its owner, perhaps of the Pelham family.

Assessing these vervels against their likely chronology (using refined dates) – Type Ciii (1536-92), Type Ci-ii (1577-1637), Type A (1609-52) and Type B (1619-64) – it seems as though the use of a pictorial device marking owners was gradually phased out in favour of a written inscription that gave both the owners' name and place of residence; although if birds were being flown in areas of well-known landed gentry then the place name might be superfluous. Perhaps with wider social ownership of the highest-grade hunting birds (and therefore ones where the owners also invested in a vervel to mark their ownership), and the increasingly complicated nature of heraldic arms – itself because of a larger aristocratic class in the Stuart period – it became increasingly necessary to have an inscription that more clearly named the bird's owner and place of residence.

Vervels therefore might indirectly comment upon social change between the late medieval and early post-medieval periods, where there is a growing aristocratic class (thanks to royal patronage thereof) and changes in the use of their landholdings, reflecting more efficient use of the land that was to advance considerably with the agrarian revolution. It is likely that hawking – prior to developments in ordnance, especially for hunting – reflected the gentrification of a wider (though still high-status) social group, that found pleasure in 'traditional' – might it be said medieval inspired – rural pursuits. This, to some extent, is reflected in the names of individuals inscribed upon the vervels listed in the catalogue below. Although these include kings, princes, earls and other high-raking aristocrats, others are of lower (albeit not insignificant) social status – some being otherwise anonymous from the historical records – implying an increased ownership of hunting birds, though we do not know what species these might have been used with.

Vervels and Hunting Birds

Documentary sources, including those described above, show that the hunting birds kept by aristocrats and landed gentry in the 17th century were of significant variety, and this also appears to have been the case in the Middle Ages.

Often referred to in relation to the social hierarchy of the ownership of hunting birds in the medieval period is the aforementioned *Book of St Albans* or *The Book of Hawking, Hunting and Blasing of Arms*, attributed to Juliana Berners (born c.1388), said to be prioress of St Mary, Sopwell, because of the inscription 'explicit dam Julyans Barnes in her boke of huntyng' at the end of the 1486 edition. The hawking treatise part of the book is thought to have been adapted from the *Booke of Hawkyng after Prince Edwarde Kyng of Englande* (British Library, Harley 2340) of the first half of the 15th century. Important here, is that *The Book of St Albans* lists the social ranks for which birds of prey were (supposedly) appropriate. This list might be untypical – even invented (especially as some birds it mentions, such as buzzards, are unlikely to have been employed in falconry) – and some bird species might be listed in error, or described with terms that are different to those used nowadays; an example here might be to equate 'lanners' with lanner falcons (see Evans 1988, 80ff). However, taken at face value, *The Book of St Albans* implies a wide social ownership of hunting birds, and that the ownership of certain species of birds was also restricted. Some of this is probably explained by the simple fact that some birds of prey were much more expensive to own than others.

The *Book of St Albans* gives the following social rankings for bird ownership:

- Emperor: eagle, vulture and merlin
- King: gyr falcon and the tercel of the gyr falcon (Fig. 14)
- Prince: 'gentle falcon'
- Duke: falcon of the loch
- Earl: peregrine falcon
- Baron: buzzard (maybe a harrier, or perhaps a 'bastard' hawk)

Fig. 14: A close-up photograph of a gyrfalcon (© Michael Lewis).

- Knight: sacre (saker falcon) and sacret (this seems unlikely due to the cost of these birds)
- Squire: lanere (lanner) and lanneret
- Lady: marlyon (possibly merlin)
- Young man: hobby
- Yeoman: goshawk
- Poor man (perhaps lower level landowner): tercel
- Priest: sparrowhawk
- Holy water clerk: sparrowhawk
- Knave/servant: kestrel

By the Renaissance, the types of hunting birds owned by aristocrats is much clearer, thanks to the relative wealth of written information about them.

The *Household Book* of the L'Estrange family of Hunstanton Hall, Norfolk, has various entries that reference the purchase, keeping and training of hunting birds, as well as other expenses associated with falconry between the years 1519 and 1579. Birds kept include 'peregrines, goshawks, hobbies, and sparrowhawks, for whose care and training a falconer was kept' (ibid.).

By the beginning of the 17th century, Edmund Bert (1619), in his *Approved Treatise on Hawkes and Hawking*, discusses hunting on the Sussex Downs with this 'intermewed' goshawk where in five weeks was killed 'four score and odd partridges, five pheasants, seven rayles, and four hares'. Gladys Scott Thompson's (1940: 228) *Life in a Noble Household*, writes about the Russell family later in the century, that 'hawks of every kind were found in those [their] mews'. These included the short-winged hawks, or goshawks, and the long-winged birds who were falcons proper. Also listed 'were the brook hawks kept especially for hunting the duck and water fowl and others of every possible variety for pursuing other game, brought from Scotland and Ireland, from Nova Scotia and New England, while North Africa supplied the swift-flying desert hawks'. Thompson also lists some excerpts from the account books, where goshawk, lanner, tercel and haggard are mentioned.

In many other sources, such as the Calendar of State Papers, Domestic (CoSD) for James I (r.1603-25), for example, references are made to generic species, such as 'hawks' and 'falcons' rather than anything more specific. Generally specific species seem to be goshawks and lanners.

It is important to note that the size and type of bird influenced the prey that it was set to pursue, and therefore the style of hunting. Although we have used the terms 'falconry' and 'hawking' interchangeably, they could technically be applied to the style of hunting using these respective families of birds. Falcons (belonging to the family *Falconidae*) are usually distinguished by their dark eyes, longer wings and relatively shorter tails. They are particularly suited to attacking other birds by flying above them and 'stooping' down upon their prey at speed, knocking it violently from the sky. This means that falconry requires an abundance of open ground, allowing for the birds to soar to a suitable elevation and for their handlers to follow them over long distances (Glassier 1998: 20-1). A particularly popular form of hunting with falcons in the medieval and post-medieval periods was to fly them at birds like herons and cranes (the latter of which were much more numerous than they are in modern times). Falcons gain altitude by steadily circling their much larger victims, then stooped down upon them, often multiple times, while the more ungainly bird sought to outdistance its pursuer. Hawks (family *Accipitridae*) have yellow eyes and relatively shorter wings, but longer tails, which makes them more skilled at negotiating low-lying obstacles (tree branches). They kill their prey with powerful talons and are particularly useful at attacking low-flying birds like pigeons or pheasants or ground-based animals like rabbits, and can be launched 'off the fist' when prey is spotted (ibid: 34). The Museum of Falconry in Valkenswaard, the Netherlands, features life-sized dioramas of both styles of hunting.

In very broad terms, the sources of the 16th and 17th centuries suggest that goshawks, lanner and peregrine falcons, were the favoured larger birds of aristocrats, with the prized smaller birds being hobbies and sparrowhawks.

Given that hawking birds vary in size and weight, and so do vervels, it might be possible to link different types of vervels to specific bird species (Table 1). Here it is hypothesised (though in very general terms) that the ring size makes the vervel suitable for a specific species of bird of prey, and indeed that some types of vervels (specifically Types B, Ci, Cii and D) were perhaps more likely to be fastened around the bird's foot, whilst others (Types A and Ciii) were fixed to the bird's jesses.

Type A vervels vary in diameter from 10mm (**A28**) to 17.3mm (**A01**), a difference of 7.3mm (Graph 8). The mean average is 12.67mm and the median is 12.11mm. As such these are amongst the largest vervels, of which Type D is the greatest. It might be significant that the largest hawking ring of this type (**A01**) belonged to a bird owned by a prince (perhaps Edward V), and the third largest (**A30** at 16mm)

Table 1: Common Hunting Birds – dimensions

Species	Body length	Wing span	Modern ID ring diameter[a]	Mass (M/F)
Sparrowhawk (Eurasian)	28–38cm	58–77cm	7.6mm	110/185–196/342g
Merlin	28–33cm	60–67cm	7.6mm	155/190–180/220g
Kestrel (Eurasian)	33–38cm	68–82cm	7.6mm	163–290g
Hobby (Eurasian)	29–36cm	74–84cm	7.6mm	175–285g
Peregrine	38–45cm	90–105cm	11.0-12.7mm	580/720–860/1090g
Lanner	44–49cm	100–110cm	12.7mm	500/700–600/900g
Goshawk (northern)	50–60cm	100–115cm	11.0-12.7mm	580/870–880/1320g
Saker Falcon	47–55cm	110–126cm	12.7mm	700/970–900/1300g
Gyrfalcon	50–60cm	110–128cm	14.3mm	960/1400–1300/2000g

[a]Taken from the website 'Identity Rings Europe', id-rings.eu. Where two values are listed, they are for the male (smaller) and female varieties.

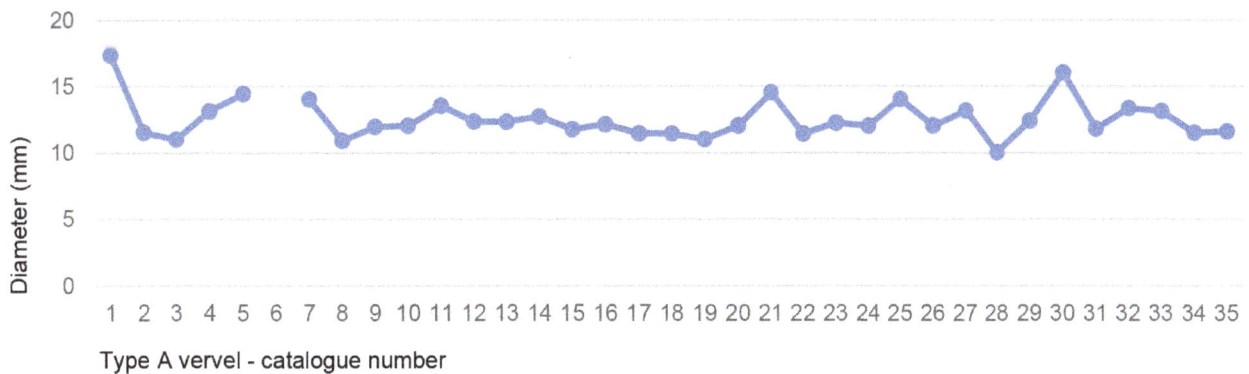

Graph 8: Type A vervels – ring diameter (external) mm.

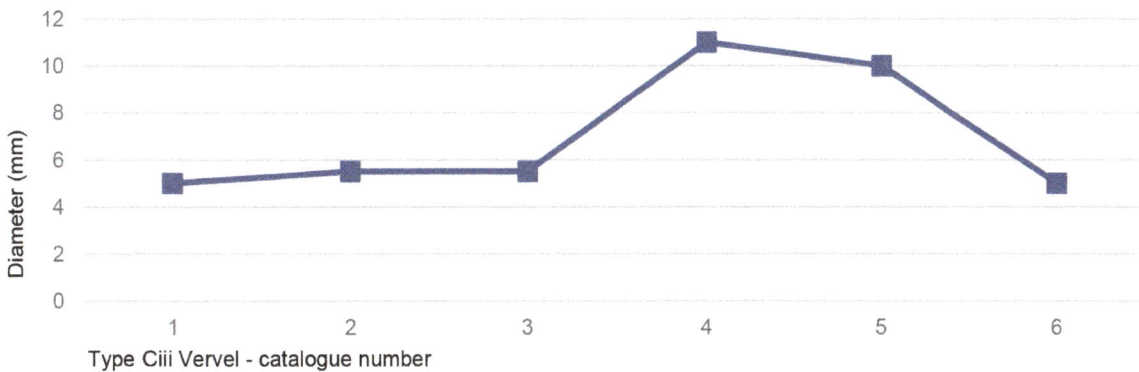

Graph 9: Type Ciii vervels – ring diameter (external) mm.

is also of late medieval date. Perhaps it can be inferred that these items were for larger birds, such as gyrfalcons, goshawks, peregrines and lanner falcons, though if they were affixed to the bird's jesses (as seems likely) then the ring diameter is of little consequence, so long as the centre hole is large enough for the leather to pass through.

Based on their form (with the shield protruding beneath an integral ring), Type Ciii vervels are likely to have functioned in a similar way to those of Type A hawking rings. There are only six of this Type, all found in the eastern counties of England, varying between 5mm (**Ciii01**) and 11mm (**Ciii04**) in internal ring diameter, a

difference of 6mm (Graph 9). The mean average of these is 7mm and the median is 5.5mm. These vervels are therefore (on average) a smaller vervel type than Type A, which may (or may not) have reflected how they were used; perhaps it suited different species of bird to have rings attached to their jesses, rather than the bird's legs.

Type B vervels seem more likely to be linked to a particular species of hunting bird (than Type A or Type Ciii hawking rings) since they are ring shaped and thus (presumably) worn over a bird's leg. They vary in size between 5.9mm (**B21**), which is unusually small, and 10.72mm (**B20**), which is quite large for this type – a difference of 7.06mm

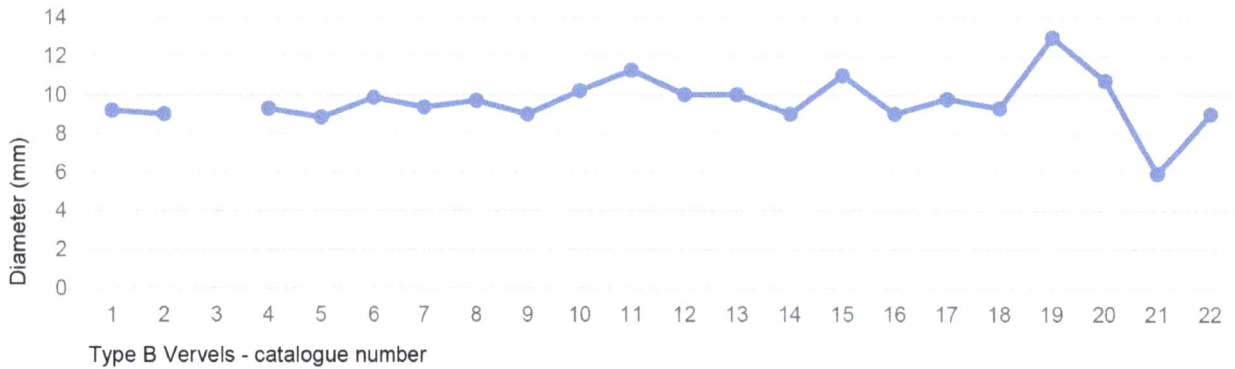

Graph 10: Type B vervels – ring diameter (external) mm.

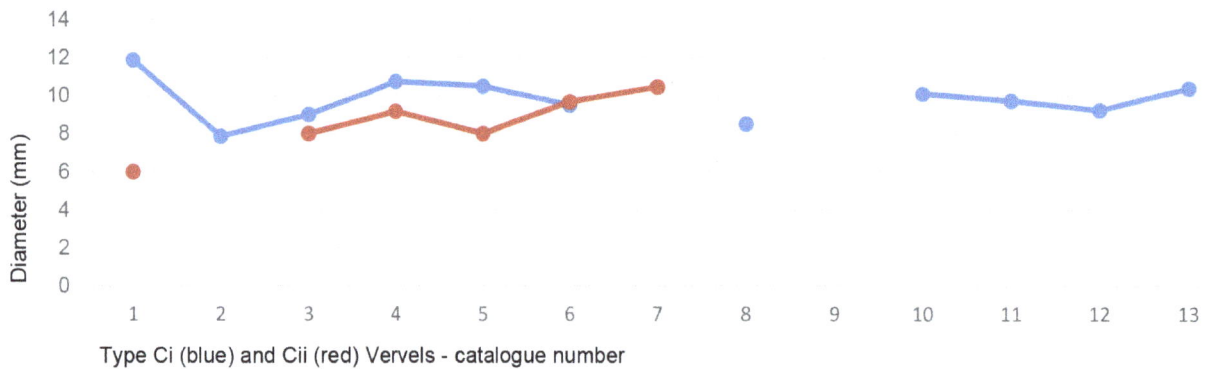

Graph 11: Type Ci and Cii vervels – ring diameter (external) mm.

(Graph 10). Their mean average diameter is therefore 9.66mm and the median being 9.36mm. The implication, therefore, is these are designed for smaller birds, such as hobbies or sparrowhawks, assuming the ring is worn over the bird's leg.

Types Ci and Cii vervels are essentially ring-shaped, so very much like Type B vervels in that respect, but with a shield attached, either vertically (Ci) or horizontally (Cii) to the external face of the ring; this is usually soldered.

Type Ci vervels vary in size between 7.85mm (**Ci02**) and 11.88mm (**Ci01**), a difference of 4.03mm. Their mean average is 9.76mm, with a median of 9.73mm. Type Cii vervels vary in size between 6mm (**Cii01**) – which is unusually small – and 10.47mm (**Cii07**), with a difference of 4.47mm. The mean average for Type Cii vervels is 8.66mm, and the median is 9.17mm (Graph 11). Type Cii vervels are therefore slightly smaller than Type Ci examples, with both types being broadly similar in size to Type B vervels – in fact Type B vervels are sized between Types Ci and Cii. It seems probable, therefore, that all were used in the same way, probably on similar sized birds.

That said, it might be that the shields on Type Ci and Cii vervels were not suitable for fixing directly to a bird's leg, and therefore this type was affixed instead to the animal's jesses, as with Type A. Indeed, the only depiction of a Type Cii vervel in art, in the aforementioned *Bestiary* of

the Holy Roman Emperor, Rudolf II of Habsburg, shows it upon the bird's jesses. Another possibility is that they were affixed in the manner of hawking bells, with a separate leather bewit.

As vervels vary in their dimensions (Graph 12), this is also reflected in their weight.

The weight of Type A vervels vary between 0.3g (**A03**) and 2.2g (**A01**), a significant difference (of 1.9g), especially as only a few of them weigh more than 1g: 2.2g (**A01**), 1.15g (**A21**), 1.1g (**A05**) and 1.06g (**A07**). Their mean weight average is therefore 0.78g, and the median being 0.7g (Graph 13).

Type B vervels vary in weight between 0.5g (**B02**) and 1.34g (**B21**), a weight variation of 0.84g. This gives a mean weight average of 0.73g, and a median one of 0.6g (Graph 14). Surprisingly, perhaps, given Type A vervels tend to be larger and possibly functioned quite differently, Type B vervels have a very similar weight average – in fact their median weight is almost the same.

Type Ci vervels vary in weight, between 0.54g (**Ci06**) and 1.8g (**Ci13**), giving a weight difference of 1.26g. Their mean average is 1.1g, with a median average of 1.04g, so they are significantly heavier than both Type A and Type B vervels. Likewise, Type Cii vervels are comparatively heavier than Type Ci, weighing between 0.84g (**Cii04**) and 1.64g (**Cii02**), with a difference of

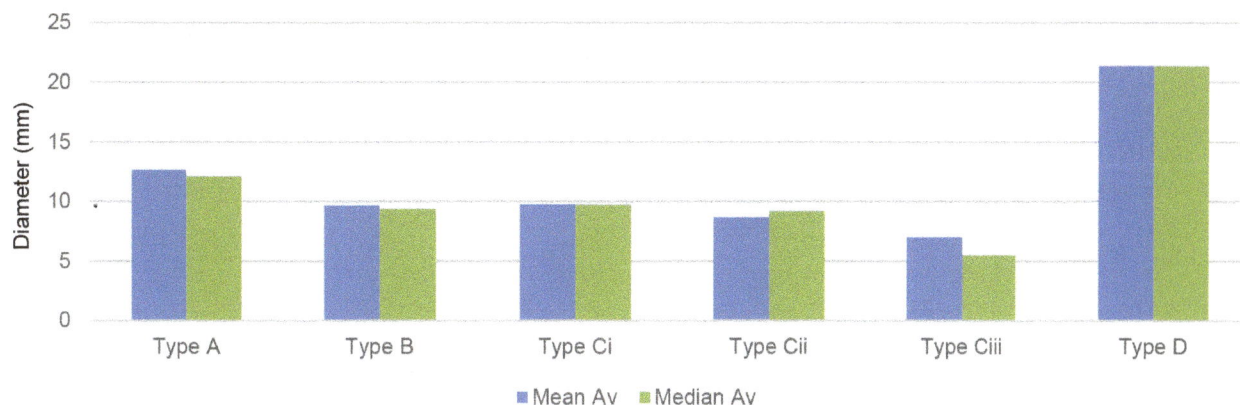

Graph 12: Vervels – ring diameter (external) mm.

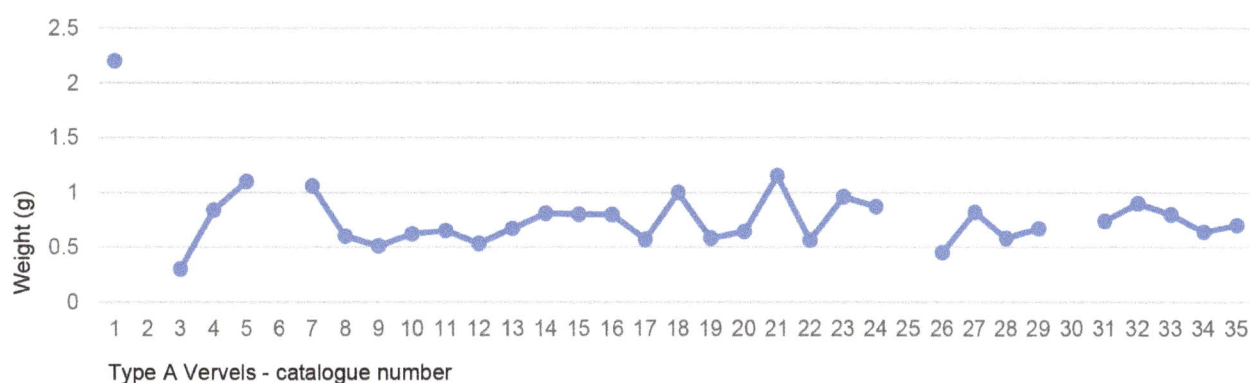

Graph 13: Type A vervels – weight.

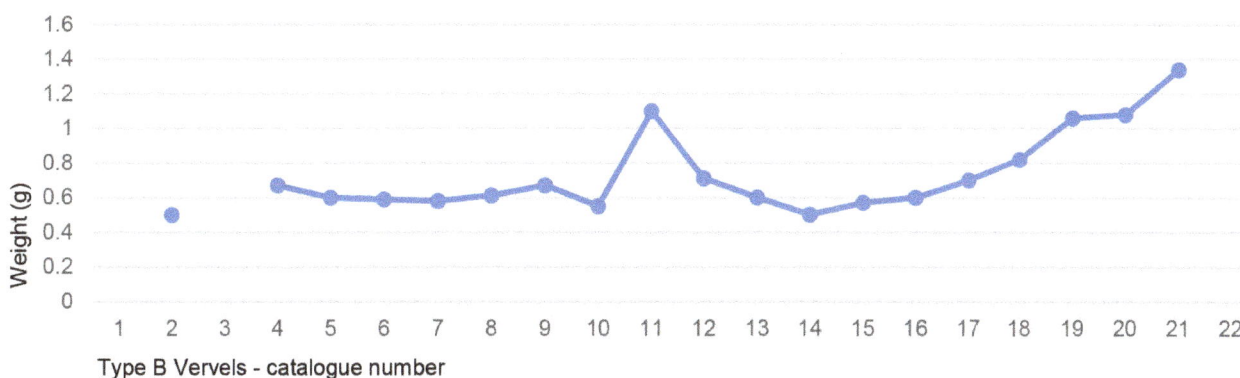

Graph 14: Type B vervels – weight.

0.8g. Their mean weight average is 1.3g, with a median of 1.5g (Graph 15). This is of interest given that it might be assumed that Type Ci and Type Cii vervels are used in a similar way, perhaps giving credence to the possibility (indicated above) that Type Cii vervels might also be attached to the bird's jesses.

Although Type Ciii vervels vary considerably in weight, between 0.46g (**Ciii06**) and 2.87g (**Ciii04**), with a massive overall difference of 2.47g, they are also (generally speaking) a heavy type; their mean weight average is 1.48g, with a median of 1.28g.

The only Type D 'garter' vervel (**D01**) weighs 1.53g and is incomplete, and therefore little meaningful can be said

about it, but if it represents half a vervel then (at 3.06g) it is heavy for this object type.

Examined together, it is apparent that Type A and B vervels are (in very general terms) lighter than those of Type C, although there is a considerable variation of weight within each type; this is perhaps unsurprising, given that Types C have the addition of a shield device to the ring (Graph 16). The practical impact of this shield element is probably worthy of some consideration, as it might have risked snagging the bird if it perched out in the wild, though perhaps the risk was minimal, or at least counterbalanced by the risk of losing an unmarked bird, especially if the item was fixed to the bird's leg, rather than trailing on jesses: a reminder, it is proposed here that Types B and D,

21

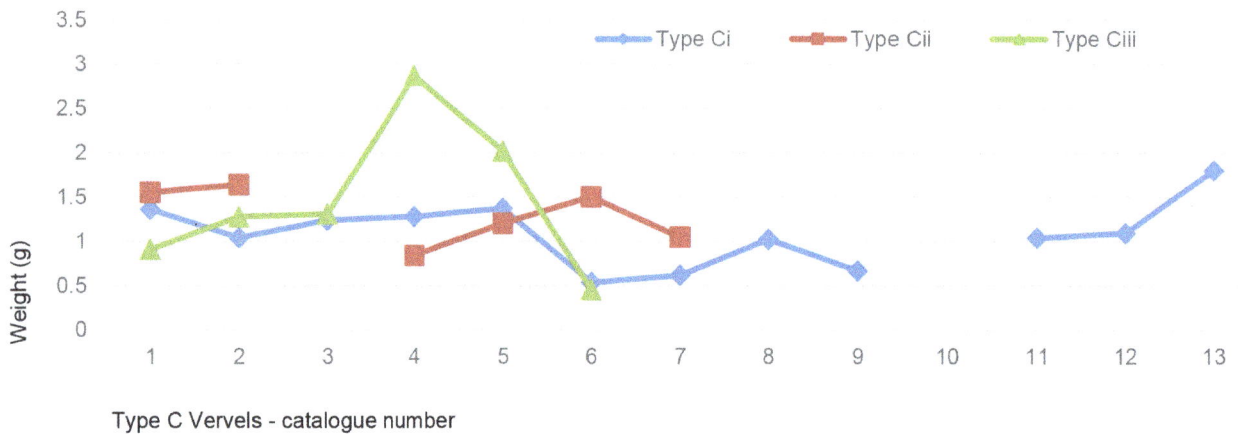

Graph 15: Type C vervels – weight.

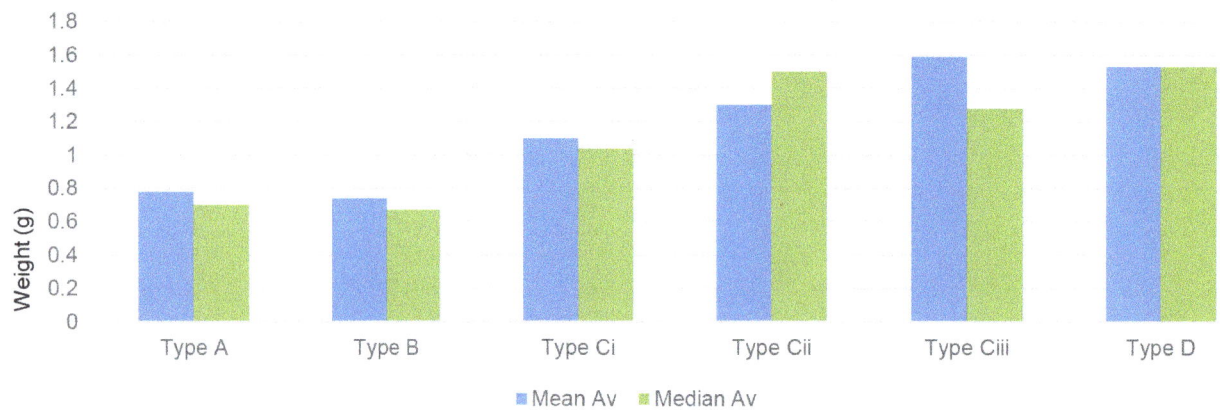

Graph 16: Vervels – weight.

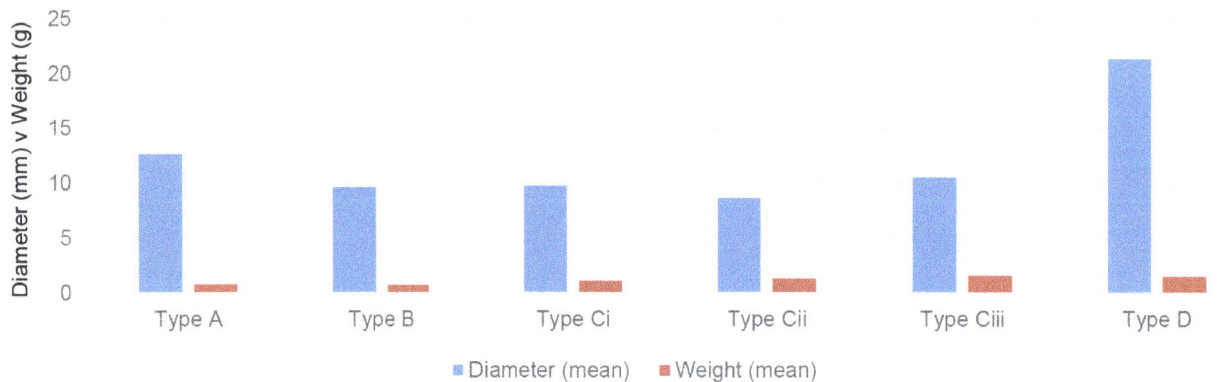

Graph 17: Vervels – ring diameter v weight.

and maybe Types Ci-ii, were fixed to a bird of prey's leg, while Types A and Ciii were fixed to a bird's leather jesses. A further consideration is whether the weight of some vervels would add a significant weight burden to a bird in flight. Although this appears to be unlikely – after all we are discussing very powerful creatures (Leigh Holmes, *pers. comm.*) – it is nonetheless possible that flying birds with extra hawking equipment might be a consideration in certain circumstances.

In summary, vervel types might be ordered by size, smallest to the largest (excluding Type D): Type Ciii (mean 7mm to median 5.5mm), Type Cii (mean 8.66mm to median 9.17mm), Type B (median 9.36mm to mean 9.66mm), Type Ci (mean 9.76mm to median 9.73mm), Type A (median 12.11mm to mean 12.67mm). Also, by their weight (lightest to heaviest): Type A (median 0.7g to 0.78g), Type B (median 0.67g to mean 0.84g), Type Ci (mean 1.1g to median 1.04g), Type Cii (mean 1.3g to median 1.5g), Type Ciii (median 1.28g to mean 1.59g). Oddly then, Type A vervels are both the largest but lightest type, perhaps suggesting this is significant to how they were used. This said the other vervel type likely to have been tied to the bird's jesses (Type Ciii) is one of the largest and the heaviest. Perhaps this suggests weight is not so much a factor for those producing vervels (Graph 17).

In terms of their chronology, we have seen that these same types can be ordered (in general terms), oldest to newest (using refined dates): Type Ciii (1536-92), Types Ci-ii (1577-1637), Type A (1609-52) and Type B (1619-64). In terms of 'speciesfication' (as implied above), it seems likely that size (rather than weight) has the most significant impact. It might therefore be suggested that for the later medieval period/early Stuart period Type Ciii (ring on jesses) were used on the larger birds, whilst Types Ci and Cii (both, plausibly rings worn on the leg, but maybe the leather jesses) were used on smaller species. Then, from the early 17th century Type A (ring on jesses) was favoured for larger raptors, and those of Type B (ring on leg) for the smaller types; although Types Ci and Cii remained in use. It is important to note that this is somewhat a generalisation, and there is likely to be some regional differences in vervel use also.

Distribution

In consideration of the locations where vervels have been found, it is important to acknowledge the factors which lead to the information used in this study (Map 1). The biases in data used by the Portable Antiquities Scheme, particularly that obtained by metal-detector users, is thoroughly discussed by Robbins (2014: 23-36), but there is a particular variable introduced when considering vervels – the nature of their loss. As mentioned earlier, it is possible that they were lost by the human handlers

of hunting birds, when in the process of changing out equipment. However it is also possible that they slipped off the bird at some point in their flight, or even that the bird itself perished and the vervels, being possibly the only inorganic materials connected to the animals, were all that survived. Added to this is that birds of prey can fly for substantial distances from the point they are released. Charles d'Arcussia (1615: 211-2) relates how one of his falcons went astray and was seen 20 leagues (about 100km) from his home, before it returned to him six months later.

Vervels are found across England, but are rare in Wales, and (it seems) unknown in Scotland and Northern Ireland. Within England they are mostly found in the southern parts of the country (from the midlands to the south) but also in the north-east, particularly Yorkshire and Lincolnshire.

A relative risk surface map of the distribution of vervels in England and Wales (Map 2), shows clustering in some areas: this compares the relative commonness of vervels against other metal-detected finds in those areas. For example, there is a notable clustering of vervels close to the North Yorkshire/County Durham border. In the west, there is a standout area of vervel finds in Herefordshire, also marking out Warwickshire and parts of Gloucestershire. In East Anglia, vervels seem to cluster in Essex, which highlights a relatively high density compared with other parts, even though more vervels are actually found in Norfolk. In Northamptonshire, in areas close to Cambridgeshire, there

All vervels to 2017

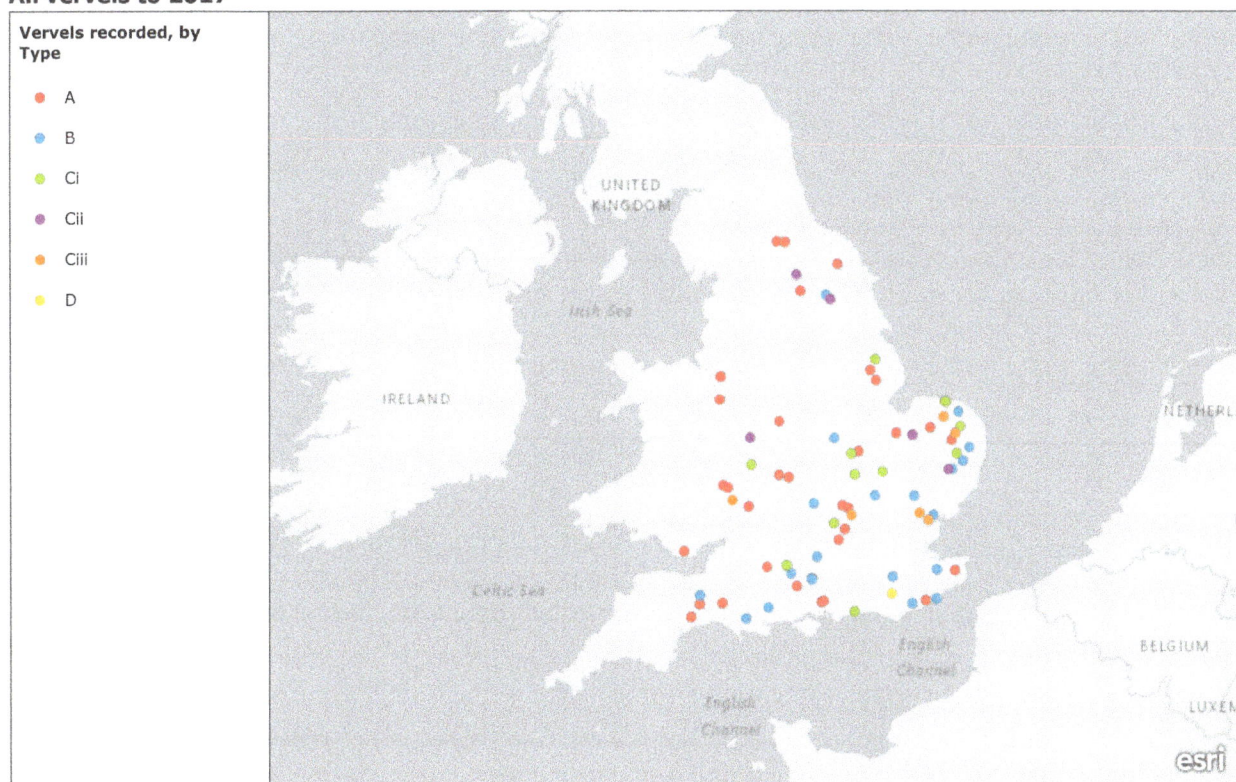

A map of all of the vervels recorded with PAS to 2017

Esri, HERE, Garmin, NGA, USGS

Map 1: All vervels in England and Wales.

seems to be a focus of vervel finds. There is also a less significant cluster to the south, in lower Bedfordshire, straddling the border with Buckinghamshire. Vervels seem to be relatively common in Kent and East Sussex, but this might not be particularly significant. Hampshire is clearly a fairly dense area for vervels (as will be discussed below), also showing a presence into Wiltshire. Vervels are not common in Dorest, but they are in comparison to other finds.

Perhaps more interesting is where vervels are not found. They are absent from the far north, such as in Cumbria and Northumbria, suggesting that the absence in Scotland is also real. They appear not to be found either in a broad band from Lancashire, through West and South Yorkshire, into Derbyshire and Nottinghamshire. They are uncommon in Cheshire and the northern Midland areas of Shropshire and Staffordshire. Also, they have not been found in London, or in Surrey or eastern parts of Berkshire, or even on the Isle of Wight. In the South West they are unknown in Cornwall or Devon.

On a local level it is apparent that some geographical areas are of particular interest, and these are worth exploring further.

At Micheldever in Hampshire there have been found four vervels, of different types (A and B) (Map 3). Most significant is a vervel (**A11**), almost certainly belonging to Lord William Russell (1639-83), found just 150m from the site of the old manor house of East Stratton; this had been inherited by William's wife, Rachel Wrothesley (c.1636-1723) upon the death of her father in 1667, two years before the couple married. The vervel can therefore be quite precisely dated, probably to 1669-83.

Close by – some 500m away – was found another (**A12**), belonging to William Wollascott of Shinfield, near Reading, Berkshire. Given Shinfield is some 38km north-east of the findspot, it is suggested that Wollascott was hawking on lands belonging to the Wrothesley-Russells, though any certain coming together of the individuals above is unrecorded. Less than 100m away from **A11** was found another vervel, though of different type (**B06**), which belonged to a hunting bird of Sir Henry Browne. He seems to have resided in East Stratton and was therefore presumably known to the Wrothesley Earls of Southampton. An almost identical vervel to **B06** – in both form, size and weight – was found 900m away on the Wrothesley's estate (**B07**), but frustratingly not giving a personal name. It has been assumed this also belonged to a hawk of Henry Browne, but this is by no means certain.

The likely dates of the vervels makes it impossible that they were all lost on the same occasion, and indeed that would have been very bad luck if it had been the case. It is probable that **B06** and **B07** (dated to c.1575-c.1625) were lost at around the same time – they could have possibly been from the same bird. **A11** was certainly lost later (as already mentioned c.1669-c.1683). In the case of **A12**,

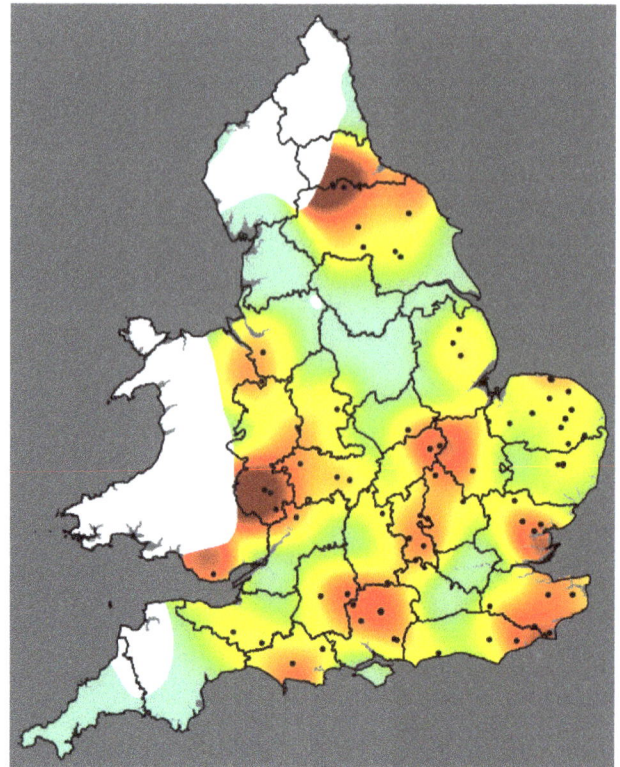

Map 2: Relative risk surface 'heat' map showing the distribution of vervels in England and Wales (Eljas Oksanen).

this has a broad date range (c.1587-c.1660), so might have been lost by William Wollascott before or after William Russell's marriage into the Wrothesleys – knowing which William Wollascott this is associated with is an added complication. Nonetheless, what is clear is that East Stratton offered prized ground for hawking, and it also attracted various individuals at several points in time. It is likely all were invited there because of their association with the Wrothesleys.

Of added interest, is the discovery of a vervel (**A10**) associated with William Russell, 5th Earl of Bedford (1616-1700), who was the father of the Lord William Russell mentioned above (associated with **A11**). This vervel was found at Kings Sombourne, some 23km south-west of East Stratton. Given the Russell family seat was at Woburn Abbey, Bedfordshire, it perhaps shows the family was attracted further south for their hawking activities.

Gladys Thompson's (1940: 232) presentation of the Bedford Estate records provides further interesting insights into the manner in which falconry was practiced amongst noble households. Writing to his son Lord Russell (1639-83) in 1672 about an upcoming visit to the former's home in Stratton Park, Hampshire, the Earl (1616-1700) said 'I shall not bring my beagles, only my hawks. Send me word whether the harvest be with you; if it be not, I will leave my hawks behind'. She also details how the Earl was invited on numerous occasions to visit the monarch for the purposes of hawking, especially at Hampton Court. The Estate records detail the expenses incurred by the Earl

Vervels from Micheldever

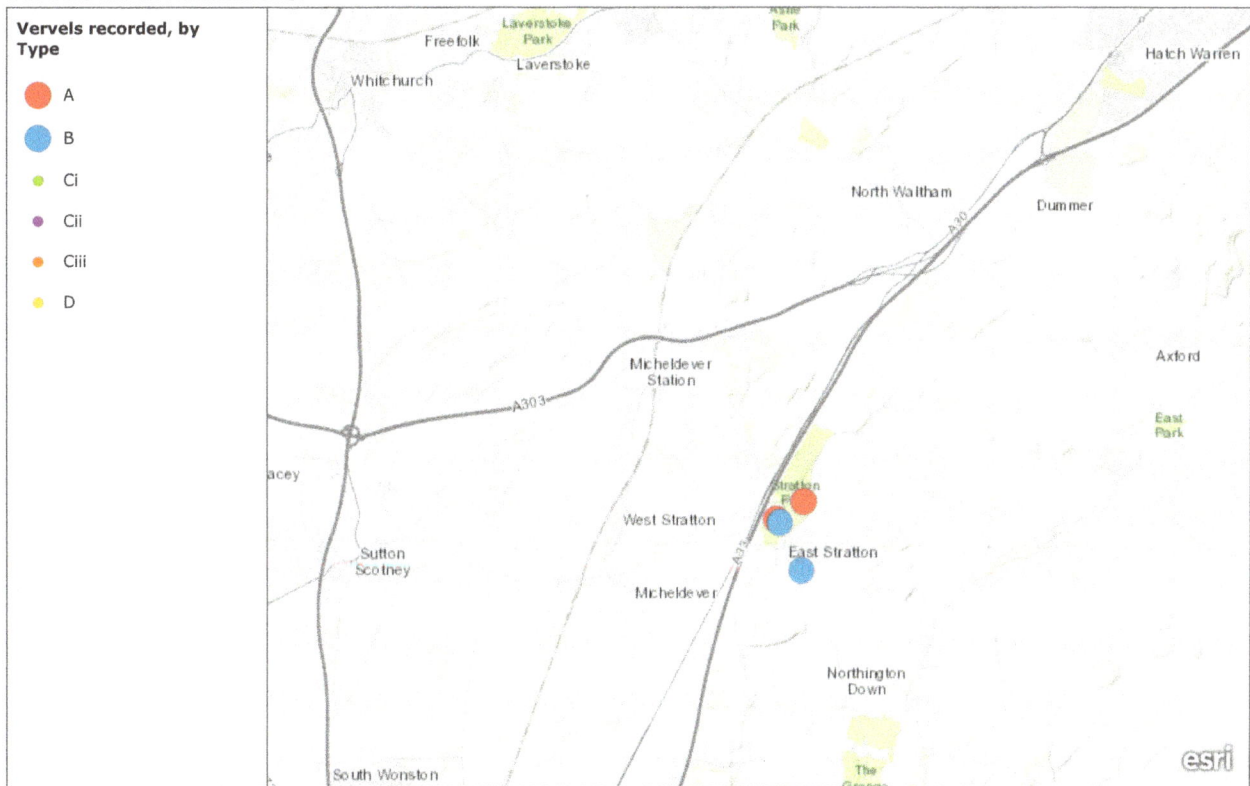

Vervels recorded, by Type

- 🔴 A
- 🔵 B
- 🟢 Ci
- 🟣 Cii
- 🟠 Ciii
- 🟡 D

Esri UK, Esri, HERE, Garmin, USGS, NGA

Map 3: Vervels from Micheldever area.

to pay for these large-scale excursions, requiring him to finance the board of several falconers and grooms and all of the necessary food for the birds. The Earl hawked not only with Charles II but also James II after the latter came to the throne, and even his successor, William III, as late as 1693 (ibid: 233). This provides us with a simple reason for the distance between the home of a named person on a vervel and its findspot.

Another notable, but seemingly unrelated, group of vervels – three in all – was found on the North Norfolk coast (Map 4). The first, from Wiveton, Norfolk (**B16**) only gives the name of a place – 'HADLYGE. IN. SVF' – so is some 100km away from whence it came. Also found at Wiveton (**Ci08**), and also travelling some distance, is a vervel reading 'Tho. Gryme. of' showing the arms of the Grimes of Trimingham, Antingham and Suffield, Norfolk. It appears to be associated with the Antingham branch of the family, so has come some 25km to be lost at Wiveton. Nearby, at Cley next the Sea (**Ci05**), was found an extremely important vervel naming Prince Henry Frederick (1594-1619), the Prince of Wales and eldest son of King James I. His association with the findspot is unknown. Interesting here is that all three are of broadly contemporary date (**B16** is dated c.1575-c.1650, **Ci08** to c.1575-c.1625, and **Ci05** to c.1600-c.1612), but are otherwise unlinked.

In examining these two concentrations of vervel findspots (Micheldever and Cley/Wiveton) it is interesting to look

at the nature of the landscapes. The Micheldever area (specifically, to the east of the village of Micheldever), is covered by the Stratton Woodlands Landscape Character Area. 'The unifying feature of this character area is the presence of woodland both locally and as a backdrop to longer views', and Stratton Park itself was home to a substantial deer park (Winchester City Council 2004: 96). The Cley/Wiveton area is comprised of a small river valley, leading down into the marshy wetlands and the sea. The vervels were found on fields at the top of the valley characterised as 'Rolling Heath and Arable' but the furthest (**Ci06**) was only just over 2km from 'Drained Coastal Marshes' which are notable for being a haven for breeding and migratory birds and for 'large skies and long views' (Land and Use Co. 2018: 194-216). The former would seem more ideal for the pursuit of woodland game whilst the latter seems an ideal habitat for waterfowl in general, and cranes and herons in particular. If that is the case we might generally expect owners to be flying hawks in the Micheldever area and falcons in Cley/Wiveton. Comparing the diameters of the type B vervels found at these locations, **B06** has a diameter of 9.86mm and **B07** is 9.36mm, while **B16** is recorded as being 9mm in diameter. If it is accepted as a possibility that this vervel type was worn directly on the legs of birds of prey, then those from Micheldever (**B06** & **B07**) appear to have come from an animal with a slightly larger leg than that connected with **B16**. But the difficulty in attributing this to a specific species is pronounced, given the variation in leg diameters

Vervels found in Cley/Wiverton

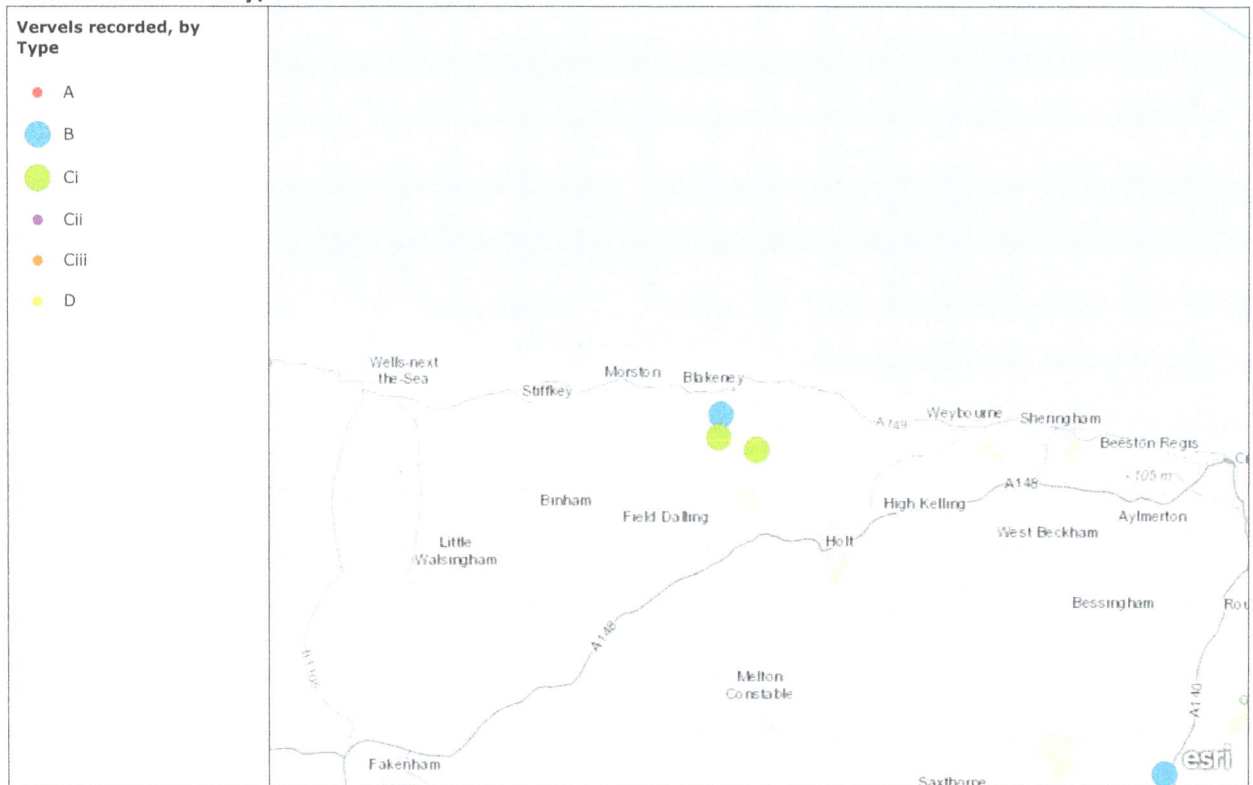

Map 4: Vervels from North Norfolk.

of both hawks and falcons. However, another interesting aspect of these two small groups of finds emerges. Those found in Micheldever consist of two Type A and two Type B vervels, whereas those from Cley/Wiveton include two Type C vervels. One reason for this could be that the more complex shape and added bulk of the C vervels made them unpopular to use in areas of heavy vegetation where they would increase the likelihood of jesses becoming tangled. The relative dearth of data makes it difficult to read much more into this and certainly is not substantial enough for us to begin to make assumptions of associations of vervel types with particular species, though that may be possible in the future with further vervel finds.

Clusters of vervels of all types around certain areas of the landscape may provide a general clue about the types of terrain over which falconry was more commonly practiced. Vervels **A07**, **A13**, **A14**, **Ci13** and **Ciii03** were all found within 3km of the River Severn or one of its major tributaries. Perhaps this is no surprise; rivers support an abundance of waterfowl and made for attractive destinations for hawking. During the Middle Ages it was common for monarchs to grant serjeanties to their hawkers and falconers which came with land adjacent to rivers (Oggins & Oggins 1992).

Other groups of vervels appear to be associated in some way with each other. At Minting, Lincolnshire were found two vervels (**A17** & **A18**) 500m apart. As stated above, both seem to refer to the same individual, George Ashton of Minting, but little certain is known about him.

Similarly, at Billesley, Warwickshire, were discovered two vervels (**A26** & **A27**) only 50m away from each other. Both name a certain Robert Lee, probably a man of that name (knighted 1608) or his son (c.1602-59). The vervels have slightly different legends – 'Sr Robert Lee // of Bilseley' (**A26**) and 'Robert. Lee + Esqr //' (**A27**), which has led to the theory that the latter (at least) is identified with the younger Robert (d.1659), since it is inscribed 'Esqr' for esquire. Indeed, a seal matrix of the younger son (WAW-5EF2D8), but made during the lifetime of his father, was found nearby. So, like the George Ashton (above), the Lees appear to be hawking on their own lands.

Conversely, at Collingbourne Kingston in Wiltshire, were found two vervels (**Ci11** & **Ci12**), which are likely to be associated with one another – indeed, they were only found 600m apart – but the owners of which have no clear link with the findspot. Both appear to show the badge of a wyvern upon a heraldic band, identified as the crest of the Herbert family, who were Earls of Pembroke. Their seat was at Wilton, so 25km to the south west of where the vervels were found. It has been suggested (see catalogue) that it is unlikely (because of their form) that the vervels were from the same bird and therefore were probably lost on different occasions. Likewise, it is assumed that the Herberts, or someone in charge of their birds, were hawking at Collingbourne Kingston, maybe as the guest of the Seymours, though an obvious local connection between remains unclear, apart from to say that wealthy aristocrats were clearly travelling some distance to fly their hawks.

Also, of intrigue are the two vervels bearing the arms of the Dukes of Norfolk, found near Witham, Essex (**Ciii02**) and in South Herefordshire (**Ciii03**), on opposite sides of England. The vervels are of such similar form and design that it seems likely that they were worked by the same hand, or (at least) modelled on a common design. That said, it is possible they could have been associated with different families, the FitzAlan Earls of Arundel or the Mowbrays. Unfortunately, nether family can be conclusively associated with the findspot, though records show that the Dukes of Norfolk travelled far and wide, of which some of this time was spent hunting with the King.

It is notable that many vervels do seem to have an immediate association with their findspot, though it can be difficult to identify (without doubt) the 'owner' named on them. Often other (sometimes circumstantial), evidence is needed to make the case. Take for example the vervel of Mr Edmund Bruning (**A08**), which does not name the place where the Brunings resided. It is only because the vervel was found at Hambledon, Hampshire, that it is possible to investigate this individual further, showing that the family came from Deanmead, Hambledon. Furthermore, some 600m from the vervel findspot is Park House, thought to be part of the Hambledon Park estate where Thomas and Richard Bruning, sons of Edmund Bruning, were born.

The immediacy of the association between a vervel and its findspot is therefore somewhat hard to judge, since it is based on a number of factors that are not equal in every case. But taking (as a broad-brush approach) those vervels that seem to identify in their inscription or imagery a family or place equal to within 2km of their findspot, it can be seen that over one third of all vervels might be said to be closely associated with their findspots. This varies slightly between vervel type: Type A (13/35) so 37%, Type B (8/22) 36% and Type C (7/26) 27%. On top of this are inscribed vervels which are found in the vicinity of aristocrat houses, which may (or may not) explain their loss.

At the other end of the spectrum are those vervels whose inscriptions link them to a person or place some distance from the findspot. Of the vervels catalogued here, 25 were found more than 10km from the place they name, or the primary place associated with the individual they name. Notable amongst these is the vervel of the Earl of Bedford (**A10**) found 135km from the place it mentions (Woburn Abbey). Broken down by type, there are 12 of Type A, 5 of Type B, and 8 of Type C, which means that roughly speaking it is just under a third of vervels that fall into this category.

What does this suggest? The purpose of a vervel, in reuniting a lost bird with its owner, is only fulfilled if the person finding the bird is able to work out who the owner might be and has some means of returning the bird to him or her. Presumably those at the higher echelons of society, like the Earls of Bedford, were distinct and important enough that they could feel confident in taking their birds a long way from home, labelled with identification linking the birds to that distant place. Indeed this seems reinforced by the evidence cited above in the correspondence of the 5th Earl of Bedford. Those lower down on the social ladder, however, might not have had the same degree of confidence in the caché of their name or the knowledge or their home manor. Surely it must be assumed that at least some of the birds carrying their vervels became lost and ended up very far from where they were being flown by their handlers.

Concluding Thoughts

Unlike many other archaeological small finds, inscribed vervels can contain important historical information which can help place them within their landscape setting. They will often name or identify their owners but might also provide information about where those people lived, travelled and hunted. However, it is only through piecing evidence together that their story of the past comes to life, and also their association with one another. Here we have attempted to bring that evidence together, but no doubt more information will come to light through further local research.

Although vervels do seem to have been used to identify the ownership of hunting birds, it is likely that they were used in different ways – some applied to the bird's legs, others to leather jesses. Such variation might also reflect the species of bird flown, as well as the locality and topography in which hunting took place. That said, the distribution of vervels does seem to suggest a common usage across England, though some areas were more favoured than others.

The evidence of the vervels listed in the catalogue show them to be mostly used in the 17th century on birds owned by aristocrats. Particularly interesting is the fact that hawking was common in the Middle Ages. Perhaps it is the case that hawking rings were not so much needed at this time, or that the birds were less prone to becoming lost.

We know that falconry was practiced by women since at least the medieval period. They appear flying birds in the *Devonshire Tapestries* for example, and on other artworks as described above, but this phenomenon is not seen in the archaeological evidence. Indeed, it would seem from the sample size of recorded vervels that women were not associated with the birds in the same way. Perhaps they partook in hawking but at the pleasure of a man, and using birds owned by them.

The end date of the vervel finds also serves as an indicator for the sharp a decline in the popularity of the sport. Perhaps since those who continued to practice falconry were so few in number it was somehow easier to track a lost bird, and so a means of identifying them was unnecessary. A further reason may also be due to biases in the Portable Antiquities Scheme data, and that more obviously recent vervels, from the 1700 and 1800s, have not been shown to Scheme's local Finds Liaison Officers because it is assumed by finders that they will not wish to record them.

The number of archaeological small finds being discovered and reported in England and Wales continues at a high level, and already there have been further vervels found which we have been unable to include in this publication. Certainly, there will be more, for years to come, and so the breadth of our knowledge will increase. What is important is that these are properly recorded, and the most significant of them acquired by local museums for study and enjoyment.

Fig. 15: Hawk being flown (©Michael Lewis).

Catalogue
Type A (Washer) Vervels

England

A01 BEDFORDSHIRE, EATON BRAY
(WMID-1738A6; 2009 T62)

Date: c.1483.

Description: Silver flat circular ring, sub-rectangular in section, inscribed on both faces in gothic script: *Prince* {three sprigs of foliage} // *Edward* {two sprigs of foliage}. 17.3mm x 1.5mm. 2.2g.

Discussion: The inscription on this vervel might be read as 'Edward Prince', though 'Prince Edward' seems much more likely. There are several princes of this name extant when this vervel was made, likely to be in the second half of the 15th century: 1) Edward 'of Westminster' (1453-71), who perished at the Battle of Tewkesbury (4 May 1471), son of Henry VI; 2) Edward V (1470-c.1483), one of the 'princes in the tower', son of Henry IV; 3) Edward 'of Middleham', Prince of Wales (1473-84), son of Richard III; 4) Edward 'Plantagenet', Earl of Warwick (1475-99), son of George, Duke of Clarence.

Of these men, only the future Edward V can be linked with Eaton Bray, where this vervel was found; although the link is somewhat tentative. Edward was at Ludlow Castle when he received news of his father's death on 14 April 1483. Ten days later he left for London via Northampton to be crowned king. At Stony Stratford, Buckinghamshire, some 30km north of Eaton Bray (on the route of Watling Street), Edward's party was intercepted by Richard, Duke of Gloucester (later Richard III). Some of Edward's men were arrested and his escort was dismissed. Thereafter Richard escorted the new king to London via Watling Street. It is upon this journey south that the royal party, or the dismissed escort, passed Eaton Bray, less than 5km east of the findspot.

It is the Bray family that gives its name to Eaton Bray. Sir Reginald Bray (c.1440-1503), whose father Richard was of Eaton Bray, was principle negotiator in arranging Henry VII's marriage to Edward's V's sister, Elizabeth 'of York', in 1486.

Location: Returned to finder/landowner.

M Lewis, J Robinson & D Slarke

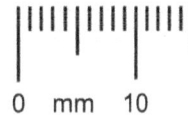

Vervel from Eaton Bray (WMID-1738A6) (courtesy of the Portable Antiquities Scheme).

King Edward V, oil painting (© National Portrait Gallery).

A02 BERKSHIRE, BISHAM (BUC-4A6CC2)

Date: c.1600-c.1700.

Description: Silver flat circular ring, sub-rectangular in section, inscribed on both faces in italic script: *{five-pointed star, cross of four dots} Esq of Bisham in // {two five-pointed stars} Berckshr.* 11.5mm x 0.97mm.

Discussion: This vervel was found close to the site of Bisham Abbey, and its extant mid-13th century manor house; the abbey was dissolved in 1536, re-founded in 1537, and dissolved again in June 1538. During the 17th century the manor was owned by the Hoby family, which took for their crest a hobby, a bird-of-prey with a pun on their name. Their ancestral line included Sir Edward Hoby MP (1560-1617), Peregrine Hoby MP (1602-79), Sir Edward Hoby (1634-75), 1st Baronet of Bisham (from 1666), and Sir John Hoby (1635-1702), 2nd Baronet of Bisham (from 1675).

Location: Returned to finder; not Treasure as found prior to the Treasure Act 1996.

M Lewis, E Ghey & R Tyrrell

Vervel from Bisham (BUC-4A6CC2) (courtesy of the Portable Antiquities Scheme).

A03 BUCKINGHAMSHIRE, BURCOTT
(BUC-88AA68)

Date: c.1626-c.1642.

Description: Copper-alloy flat circular ring, sub-rectangular in section, inscribed on both faces in italic script: *{six-pointed star} A. Pitcairne. at. Cortt // {six-pointed star} keper.*. 11mm x 0.7mm. 0.3g. Inscribed copper-alloy vervels are excessively rare, this being the only example recorded with the PAS.

Discussion: The inscription may be transcribed as 'A. Pitcairne, at Court, keeper', and bears the name of Andrew Pitcairn (d.1642) who was Chief Falconer to King Charles I from at least May 1625 (NA: SP/14/214 f.109). Pitcairn was the youngest son of Henry Pitcairn (c.1560-1626), 15th lord of the Perthshire Pitcarns of Kintillo, and became *servitor* to Prince Charles in 1612, when he was Duke of York.

The vervel was found less than 1km from Ascott House (HE: 1291467). In the 17th century, Ascott House was home to the Dormer family. Robert Dormer (1551-1616), 1st Baron Dormer (from 1615) and his grandson of the same name (1610-43), 2nd Baron Dormer, later 1st Earl of Carnarvon (from 1628), and owner of **Ci02** (below), were both Master of the Kings Hawks. Upon the restoration of Charles II (1660), Andrew Pitcairn's son, Charles, petitioned the Crown for a sum of £2,000 on behalf of a debt owed to his family when his father sold his place of Master Falconer to Earl Carnarvon for the fee of £5,000, which had not been paid (CoSD, Charles II, May 1660: no. 178); Carnarvon was known to be addicted to gambling and hunting, and was killed at the Battle of Newbury.

Location: Returned to finder/landowner.

I Richardson, M Lewis, R Tyrell & J Moss

Vervel from Burcott (BUC-88AA68) (courtesy of the Portable Antiquities Scheme).

Robert Dormer, engraving in the British Museum (©The Trustees of the British Museum).

A04 BUCKINGHAMSHIRE, LITTLE MISSENDEN
(BUC-D9DCD5; 2016 T645)

Date: c.1600-c.1700.

Description: Silver flat circular ring, sub-rectangular in section, inscribed on both faces in italic script: *In. the. County // {eight-pointed star} of {cross} Buckinghame.* 13.1mm x 1.1mm. 0.84g. The recorder has noted that there is a patch of black corrosion between the words 'county' and 'in' on the obverse, apparent (but less so) on the reverse also.

Discussion: The nature of the inscription upon this vervel suggests that it might be one of a pair, the other giving the name of the bird's owner; without it such an inscribed vervel would have served little practical purpose in helping to identify the ownership of lost hunting birds.

Close to the findspot are several 17th century buildings, such as Beamond End Farmhouse (HE: 1124920), Chabot (HE: 1310001) and Stud Cottage (HE: 1124988). Most significant, however, is Woodrow High House (HE: 1311156), which is located approximately 1300m south-east of the findspot. The current building is early 18th century and later, but incorporates the fabric of an earlier house, known as Woodside House, once owned by the Drake family; it is reputed that Oliver Cromwell's wife and daughters were said to have lived here at times during the English Civil War. For much of the 17th century Woodside House was home to Sir William Drake (1606-69), 1st Baronet of Shardeloes (from 1641), who inherited the Amersham estates in 1626. He was succeeded by his nephew, also called William (1651-90). Both men were MPs for Amersham (between 1640-8, 1661-9 and 1669-89).

Location: Buckinghamshire County Museum.

M Lewis, I Richardson & A James

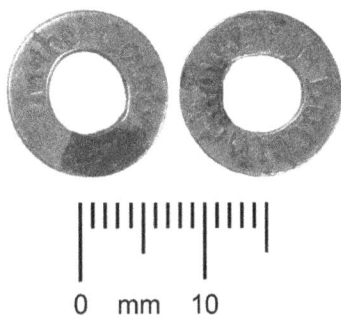

Vervel from Little Missenden (BUC-D9DCD5) (courtesy of the Portable Antiquities Scheme).

A05 CHESHIRE, BRUEN STAPLEFORD (PUBLIC-A42D62; 2013 T536)

Date: c.1575-c.1637.

Description: Silver flat circular ring, sub-rectangular in section, inscribed on both faces in italic script: *{cross, arms a burst of three dashes} J: Bruen of {cross, arms a burst of three dashes} // {burst of five dashes} Stapleford in {bust of five dashes}.* 14.4mm x 0.8mm. 1.1g.

Discussion: This vervel may have been one of a pair (see A04 for example), with the second inscribed 'Cheshire', or such like. It probably belonged to a hunting bird of John Bruen (1560-1625) of Stapleford Hall (extant building is HE: 1130558), who was the son of a Cheshire squire of Bruen Stapleford, and in later life a well-known Puritan (see DNB); the object was found some 600m away from the site of the family home. Rev William Hinde (1857: 23), Bruen's biographer, discussed how 'in the prime of his life (about the twenty-first year of his age), John Bruen was much addicted to the ordinary exercises and recreations of hunting and hawking', but he gave these up upon inheriting his father's estates in 1587. The inscription upon the vervel suggest a 17th century date, so it is possible that the object instead names one of Bruen's sons, probably his namesake, John (1584-1647); another son, James (1587) died in infancy.

Location: Grosvenor Museum, Chester.

I Burton, I Richardson & M Lewis

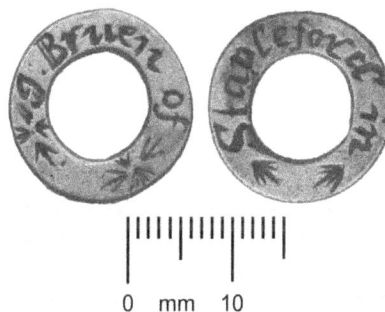

Vervel from Bruen Stapleford (PUBLIC-A42D62) (courtesy of the Portable Antiquities Scheme).

J. BRVEN

John Bruen of Stapleford, engraving in the British Museum (©The Trustees of the British Museum).

A06 DEVON, OTTERY ST MARY (DEV-6141DD; 2017 T876)

Date: c.1646-c.1686.

Description: Silver flat circular ring, sub-rectangular in section, inscribed on both faces in italic script: *Returne to Gilbert . Hodey // {six-pointed star} of Alscot [foliate sprig] in Devon*; a slight change in the surface on both sides at 1-2 o'clock seems to suggest the loop was soldered closed at this point. 14.1mm x 1.3mm. 1.10g.

Discussion: This vervel appears to belong to Gilbert Hody of Cornworthy, Devon, descended from both Sir John Hody (d.1441) and, his son, Sir William Hody (d.1524). The family home was at Nethway (also known as Nithway), near Brixham; presumably on the site of Nethway House (HE: 1146591). Gilbert Hody purchased Alscot (also known as Alverdiscott), Devon, from Sir Arthur Nothcott (1628-88), and when he died (in 1686) he left two daughters as his heiresses (Westcote 1845: 293). There is a fine memorial to Gilbert Hody 'of Nethway' (d.1686) in All Saints, Alverdiscott.

The vervel was found some 48 miles south-east of Alverdiscott (also some 40 miles north-east of Nethway), near to Ottery St Mary, at Alfington. There are listed buildings in the vicinity of the findspot, some dating to the 17th century (e.g. HE: 1212711 & 1365710), but none are clearly associated with the Hody family. North-west of Ottery St Mary, though 4km from the findspot, is Cadhay House (HE: 1289400), a 16th century building on the site of an even earlier mansion, but restored in the Georgian period, and the home of the Haydon family. Perhaps the Haydons and Hodys were known to one another, which might explain the loss of the vervel.

Location: Museum of Barnstaple & North Devon hopes to acquire.

M Lewis, L Burnett & W Partridge

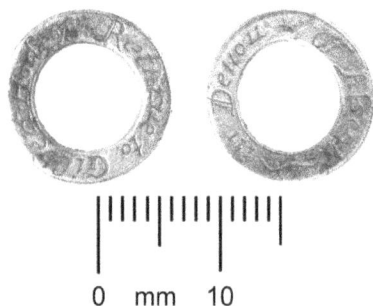

Vervel from Ottery St Mary (DEV-6141DD) (courtesy of the Portable Antiquities Scheme).

A07 GLOUCESTERSHIRE, HARTPURY (GLO-21058E; 2015 T338)

Date: c.1600-c.1700.

Description: Silver flat circular ring, rectangular in section, inscribed on both faces in italic script: *{three vertical dots} morton county worsester // esy*. 14mm x 1.4mm. 1.06g.

Discussion: The inscription upon this vervel refers to the place of residence of the owner, Abbots Morton in Worcestershire, though it is not known what 'esy' stands for. It is possible that the vervel was originally intended to feature the owner's name as well, and the 'esy' should have read 'esq' as seen on other vervels (see **A02** and **B18**, for example).

Still extant at Abbots Morton is the 'old manor' house (HE: 1096331) of early 17th century date. This is situated close to a medieval moated site (HE: 1016940) known to be favoured by the bishops of Evesham; itself adjacent to St Peter's church (HE: 1350229). After the Dissolution the site, like much of the lands of Evesham, passed into the Hoby family, but by 1600 ownership of the manor of Abbots Morton was disputed; in 1597 Philip Kighley had married Elizabeth Hoby (daughter of Richard Hoby), and thereby claimed Abbots Morton, a claim complicated by his death and her remarriage.

The vervel was found close to the moated site of Hartpury Court (HE: 1016832), upon which a mid-19th house (HE: 1172186), replacing an earlier structure, now stands; early buildings close by include the tithe barn (HE: 1172209) and St Mary's church (HE: 1078669). In 1547 the property was leased to Richard Pates, but thereafter, until 1794, its history is not recorded. Consequently, it has not been possible to trace the sometime owner of this vervel.

Location: Returned to finder/landowner.

K Adams & M Lewis

Vervel from Hartpury (GLO-21058E) (courtesy of the Portable Antiquities Scheme).

A08 HAMPSHIRE, HAMBLEDON (SUSS-60BF64; 2017 T351)

Date: c.1650-c.1706.

Description: Silver flat circular ring, sub-rectangular in section, inscribed on both faces in italic script: *Mr Edmund {trefoil}. {cross fleury}. // {cross fleury, foliate sprig, trefoil} Bruning {trefoil, foliate sprig, foliate cross}*. 10.89mm x 0.98mm. 0.6g.

Discussion: The Brunings were of Denmead in Hambledon from at least the mid-16th century, when William Wayte (d. 1561) divided his vast estates in Hampshire and the Isle of Wight between his six daughters, including Eleanor (d. 1593), who was married to Richard Bruning. Edmund Bruning appears to be of this family, but was not a direct beneficiary of the estate. Records show that in 1664, Edmund was in a long, but failed, dispute with Nathaniel Langrish (of that manor) over rights-of-way (BHO); here Edward Bruning is named as being of the manor of Rothercombe, some 12km north-east of Hambledon, where 17th century buildings still survive. It is also recorded that in 1699 Edmund and others were taken to court concerning property in Hambledon by George Higgins (NA: C 7/151/20). Edmund Bruning died in 1706 (NA: PROB 11/490/225).

Less than 1km from the findspot is Park House (HE: 1166472) of which parts date to the 16th and 17th centuries. Two of Edmund Bruning's sons, Thomas (1674-1719) and Richard (d.1720), were born at Hambledon Park, of which Park House is presumably on that estate (Monks in Motion).

Location: Hampshire Cultural Trust.

M Lewis & E Wood

Vervel from Hambledon (SUSS-60BF64) (courtesy of the Portable Antiquities Scheme).

A09 HAMPSHIRE, HORNDEAN (SUSS-035F6D; 2016 T699)

Date: c.1620-c.1662.

Description: Silver flat circular ring, sub-rectangular in section, inscribed on both faces in italic script: *{six-pointed star} Will: Englefeilde. Esq. // {six-pointed star} of. Spensers=*. 11.93mm x 1.15mm. 0.51g.

Discussion: The inscription upon this vervel probably refers to William Englefield (1609-62), the fourth son of Sir Francis (1st Baronet) Englefield (1562-1631). William's wife, Mary, is commemorated in St Mark's Church, Englefield, Berkshire, on a ledger stone, reading 'Mary Englefeild, relict of William Englefeild, Esquire, son of Sir Francis Englefeild, Bt. and daughter of Bartholomew Fromonds of Cheham, Co. Surrey, Esquire; d.1682' (Spokes 1938: 47); it is noteworthy that the name 'Englefield' is alternatively rendered as 'Englefyld' in the

same church, so it is not surprising that the spelling on the vervel also differs.

William Englefield had the manor of Hinton Markaunt in Catherington, Hampshire, conveyed to him in 1635 (BHO). The findspot, in the same village, is near to Hinton Manor House (HE: 1179041), which dates to the early 17th century and once belonged to the Hyde family.

Location: Hampshire Cultural Trust hopes to acquire.

I Richardson, M Lewis & E Wood

Vervel from Horndean (SUSS-035F6D) (courtesy of the Portable Antiquities Scheme).

A10 HAMPSHIRE, KINGS SOMBOURNE (HAMP3205; 2003 T58)

Date: c.1641-c.1700.

Description: Silver flat circular ring, sub-rectangular in section, inscribed on both faces in italic script: *{six-pointed star} Will: Earle of Bedford // {six-pointed star} at Wooborne Abby*. 12mm x 0.5mm. 0.62g.

Discussion: This vervel is almost certainly associated with William Russell (1613-1700), 5th Earl of Bedford (from 1641), thereafter Duke of Bedford (from 1694). His family seat was Woburn Abbey, Bedfordshire, some 135km north-east of the findspot. Prior to inheriting his peerage Russell was MP for Tavistock, during both the Short (1640) and Long Parliaments (1640-60). He sided with Parliament during the English Civil War, before briefly defecting to the Royalists (1643).

Manor Farmhouse (HE: 1167641) at Kings Sombourne, which dates to at least the 16th century, is less than 1km from the findspot. There are also other early buildings, within the settlement of Kings Somborne itself, including Old Palace Farm (HE: 1296891). It is not clear what (if any) association these buildings might have had with William Russell or his hawking ring.

Location: Returned to finder/landowner.

D Thornton, M Lewis & S Worrell

Vervel from Kings Sombourne (HAMP3205) (courtesy of the Portable Antiquities Scheme).

RUSSELL first Duke of BEDFORD 1694

William Russell, 1ˢᵗ Duke of Bedford, engraving in the British Museum (©The Trustees of the British Museum).

A11 HAMPSHIRE, MICHELDEVER (HAMP-039157; 2011 T275)

Date: c.1669-c.1683.

Description: Silver flat circular ring, sub-rectangular in section, inscribed on both faces in italic script: *Mr Will Russell of Stratton // in Hampshire.* 13.5mm x 0.65mm. 0.65g.

Discussion: This vervel almost certainly once belonged to a hunting bird owned by Lord William Russell (1639-83), the third son of the 5th Earl of Bedford (see **A10**). In 1669, William Russell married Rachel Wrothesley (c.1636-1723), who had received the manor of East Stratton from her father, Thomas, 4th Earl of Southampton, upon his death two years previously (1667). It was about 150m from the site of the manor (demolished in 1963) that this vervel was found.

William Russell was executed on 11 July 1683 at Lincoln's Inn Fields, London, for his part in the Rye House Plot, a plan to assassinate King Charles II (r. 1660-85) and his brother, James (1633-1701), Duke of York (later James

II) at Hoddesdon, Hertfordshire when the royal party was returning from horseraces at Newmarket (Lewis 2012: 324-5). William Russell was sentenced to be hung, drawn and quartered, afterwards commuted to death by beheading; he was posthumously pardoned.

Location: Hampshire Cultural Trust.

M Lewis & R Webley

Vervel from Micheldever (HAMP-039157) (courtesy of the Portable Antiquities Scheme).

The Trial of William Russell in the Old Bailey, with William Russell on the witness stand (©The Trustees of the British Museum).

A12 HAMPSHIRE, MICHELDEVER (SUR-D32343; 2012 T290)

Date: c.1587-c.1660.

Description: Silver-gilt flat circular ring with sub-rectangular slot cut into internal edge, rectangular in section, inscribed on both faces in italic script: *{cross} Williã {cross} Wollascott {five-pointed star} of Shinfelde // {five-pointed star} near. Readinge {cross} in. Barcke.* 12.31mm x 0.93mm. 0.53g.

Discussion: This vervel is associated with the Wollascott family of Shinfield. The manor of Shinfield came into the possession of Anne Martyn, the wife of William Wollascott, in 1604, following the death of her father; there is a memorial in St Mary's Church, Shinfield (HE: 11181231) to her parents, Edward and Mary, showing Anne in prayer.

William died in 1637 (NA: PROB11/175/213), and was succeeded by his son, of the same name (d.1660); he was High Sherriff of Berkshire (1648-9), also had a son named William (dates unknown). The vervel probably relates to one of these individuals.

The manor house of Shinfield is no longer extant, but was located to the east of the modern settlement of Shinfield east of St Mary's (mentioned above), not far from the River Loddon, and some 38km north-east of the findspot. Across the road from the church is a farmhouse of late 15th century date (HE: 1118132), with 17th century features, which may have been associated with the manor.

This vervel, was found only 500m north-east of the vervel above (**A11**), and therefore likely to be associated with a hunt organised on land belonging to the Wrothesley-Russells. To date, no written record has been found to link any of the William Wollascotts with such an event.

Location: Returned to finder/landowner, and subsequently sold at auction (2013).

D Williams & M Lewis

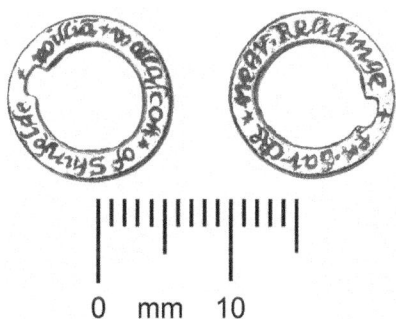

Vervel from Micheldever (SUR-D32343) (courtesy of the Portable Antiquities Scheme).

A13 HEREFORDSHIRE, MORETON
(HESH-C5E067; 2011 T395)

Date: c.1651.

Description: Silver flat circular ring, sub-rectangular in section, inscribed on both faces in italic script: *Tho : Salway of : // : Throckmorton :*. 12.3mm x 1mm. 0.67g. The vervel is notably blackened.

Discussion: This vervel probably belonged to a hunting bird owned by Thomas Salway (Salwey) of Throckmorton, Worcestershire. In 1651 Thomas became guardian to Sir Francis Throckmorton (1641-80) following the death of his father, Sir Robert (Warwickshire CR: 1998/Box86/34&46a; Broadway 2009: 141), in 1650.

Throckmorton is located some 60km east of the findspot. It is the site of a moated medieval settlement (HE: 1016938), within which an early 16th century manor house still stands (HE: 1273256). Throckmorton is connected to Moreton by the marriage of one of Thomas Salway's seven sisters, Anne, to Peter Dauncer of Moreton. No extant 17th century buildings survive in the vicinity, apart

from a barn (HE: 1172724) near to St Andrew's church (HE: 1099254). Perhaps the vervel was lost when Thomas visited Anne, or it was gifted to her and then lost.

Location: Herefordshire Museum Service (Hereford Museum & Art Gallery).

P Reavill, Z Burford & M Lewis

Vervel from Moreton (HESH C5E067) (courtesy of the Portable Antiquities Scheme).

A14 HEREFORDSHIRE, WITHINGTON area
(HESH-4DED0C; 2017 T578)

Date: c.1390-c.1450.

Description: Silver flat circular ring, sub-rectangular in section, inscribed on both faces in gothic script: *{six-pointed star} Marche // {eight-pointed star} (?G/V/B) luecrtre*. The script is in an angular black-letter hand with augmented serifs. The lettering on the upper surface is unevenly spaced. 12.7mm x 1.2mm. 0.81g.

Discussion: The meaning of the inscription on the vervel is uncertain but appears to read 'marche' (or 'marsh'), and '?luectre' may be '?luestre'. If the opening letter before 'luestre' is a 'G', then 'Gluestre' is possible (for 'Gloucester'). Based on that it has been suggested (Malcolm Jones, *pers. comm.*) that the vervel might be associated with one of two Dukes of Gloucester: Thomas of Woodstock (1385-97) or Humphrey of Lancaster (1414-47), but neither were marcher lords, as the name 'marche' may suggest. Alternatively, 'marche' or 'marsh' might be a medieval English form of modern 'marquis', but the Marquis of Gloucester is not a known title, or that it is simply a surname.

In the immediate vicinity of the findspot are a number of listed buildings, but none (apparently) dating back to the Middle Ages. However, approximately 2400m from the findspot is the site of a possible medieval settlement at Thinghill Magna (Herefordshire HER: 6534), and beyond that Thinghill Grange (HE: 1348998), which is of 14th century date. More ancient is the moated site near Hemhill (HE: 1014883), some 1800m away. Perhaps the vervel is associated with activity at one of these sites.

Location: Herefordshire Museum Service (Hereford Museum & Art Gallery) hopes to acquire.

M Jones, P Reavill, J Cherry & M Lewis

Vervel from Withington area (HESH-4DED0C) (courtesy of the Portable Antiquities Scheme).

A15 KENT, WINGHAM (KENT-DE4593; 2010 T12)

Date: c.1600-c.1700.

Description: Silver flat circular ring, rectangular in section, inscribed on both faces in italic script: {small cross} *Allinghtie neve wie // in Kent* {small cross}. 11.75mm. 0.8g.

Discussion: Efforts to decipher this vervel's inscription have failed. It has been suggested that 'neve wie' might be 'near Wye' (David Williams, *pers. comm.*), but no such village of 'Allinghtie' (or similar) exists in the vicinity; though to the east of Wye is Hastingleigh, so it is plausible that the inscription might be an adulteration of that name. Less likely is the hypothesis made by the recorder that 'neve' or 'Allinghtie' might be family names, especially given the form the inscription follows that of other vervels that only name a place, not the owner (see **A07**, above).

The vervel was found about 1200m from Goodnestone Park (HE: 1070296), the site of an early 18th century palladian house built upon that of an earlier manor. During the 17th century the manor was held by the Engeham family, including Sir Thomas Engeham (d. 1621), and his sons.

Location: Returned to finder/landowner.

J Jackson, D Thornton, D Williams & M Lewis

Vervel from Wingham (KENT-DE4593) (courtesy of the Portable Antiquities Scheme).

A16 KENT, WITTERSHAM (SUSS-7E413B; 2017 T1216)

Date: c.1600-c.1650.

Description: Silver flat circular ring, sub-rectangular in section, inscribed on both faces in italic script: *{eight-pointed star} THOMAS CRISPE: OF / GOVDHURST. IN. KENT.* The 'N' and 'T' in 'Kent' are ligated, and the letters appear to be painted red. 12.11mm x 3.03mm x 1.38mm. 0.8g.

Discussion: The individual named on this vervel is likely to be Thomas Crispe 'of Goudhurst' (c.1600-60), who was married to Anne, youngest daughter of Sir Thomas Roberts (d. 1627), baronet; this marriage gave Thomas status, though he was a gentleman in his own right. Their eldest son, also named Thomas, is recorded as succeeding to the manor of Stonar, Kent, from his uncle, Henry Crispe of Quekes (d.1663) (BHO); at All Saints, Birchington (HE: 1094681), there is a memorial to Marie Crispe (d.1618), her husband (Henry), and family, including Henry who bequeathed lands to Thomas son of Thomas Crispe of Goudhurst. On 18 November 1621 a Walter Crispe, son of Thomas Crispe, was baptised in the parish of Goudhurst and Kilndown.

Wittersham, where the vervel was found, is some 26km south-east of Goudhurst. It is recorded that the manor-house here, as Wittersham (prob. HE: 1323166), was sometime granted to Sir Henry Crispe of Quekes (d.1575), once described as 'the little king of the Isle of Thanet' (HoP), who settled it on his son, Nicholas Crispe (d 1564) (BHO), but also that it came into possession of the Crispe family through Nicholas' marriage (1549) to Frances Cheyne, daughter of Sir Thomas Cheyne (d.1558); all three men were MPs in Kent, and there is the tomb of Sir Henry in the aforementioned church of All Saints, Birchington. Upon Nicholas' death the manor passed to his daughter Dorothy, then the possession of the Bishop family and their successors. It is therefore not clear why the vervel came to be lost in Wittersham, though perhaps the Crispe family maintained a connection with that place. The findspot is 1800m away from the aforementioned manor-house, though there are 17th century buildings closer by, such as The Stocks (HE: 1070851).

Location: Returned to finder/landowner.

M Lewis & E Wood

Vervel from Wittersham (SUSS-7E413B) (courtesy of the Portable Antiquities Scheme).

A17 LINCOLNSHIRE, MINTING (WMID-16CD27; 2013 T580)

Date: c.1600-c.1700.

Description: Silver flat circular ring, sub-rectangular in section, inscribed on one face in italic script: *{six-pointed star} George Ashton of.* 11.44mm x 1.04mm. 0.57g.

Discussion: This vervel was found about 500m away from **A18**. Both objects, though slightly different in size and weight, are likely to be related to one another (see discussion below).

Location: Returned to finder/landowner.

M Lewis & T Gilmore

Vervel from Minting (WMID-16CD27) (courtesy of the Portable Antiquities Scheme).

A18 LINCOLNSHIRE, MINTING (WMID-1640D6; 2013 T579)

Date: c.1600-c.1700.

Description: Silver flat circular ring, sub-rectangular in section, inscribed on one face in italic script: *of minting lincln.* 11.42mm x 1.64mm. 1g.

Discussion: This vervel was found 500m from from **A17**. Both are inscribed on one side only, and therefore together may read *George Ashton of / of Minting Lincin* [for Lincoln or Lincolnshire]. The use of the word 'of' twice might suggest these vervels are not directly related, although it is also plausible this is an error or even purposeful. The script of each vervel differs somewhat, especially if the common letters of 'f', 'n', 'o' and 't' are studied closely, as does the metal patina; this does not necessarily preclude the fact that they were made together, or one was made to accompany the other.

On 7 October 1607, a certain George Ashton of Minting, and his wife, Mary, were named 'full executors' in the will of John Dighton (made 18 December 1606); Mary being the cousin of the deceased (Maddison 1891: 14-6). This led to a family feud for it deprived a certain Robert Dighton. Court records show that in February 1606, George and his wife were plaintiffs in a case involving 'fraud, forgery, unlawful assembly, destruction of property and contempt', against Thomas Dighton (brother of Mary Ashton), Dighton's son (Thomas) and daughter (Mary), and Robert Watson (NA: STAC 8/37/11). A similar case

was defended in June the following year (NA: STAC 8/37/12) by the aforementioned Thomas (the elder), John Holland of Hemingby and Robert Smithe of Horsington. It is not known for certain whether this vervel was owned by this George Ashton, or another namesake.

Minting is the site of Minting Priory (HE: 1004956) and some 17th century buildings, such as Priory Cottage (HE: 1063157), which is close to the findspot.

Location: Returned to finder/landowner.

M Lewis & T Gilmore

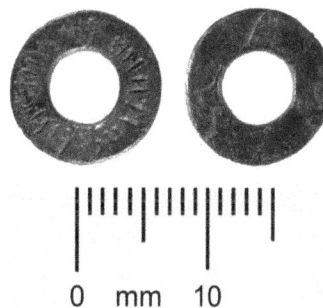

Vervel from Minting (WMID-1640D6) (courtesy of the Portable Antiquities Scheme).

A19 NORFOLK, EMNETH (NMS-2C1204; 2007 T305)

Date: c.1620-c.1660.

Description: Silver flat circular ring, rectangular in section, inscribed on one face in italic script: *m' Come. buck of Chichly.* 11mm x 1mm. 0.58g.

Discussion: The place of 'Chichly' is not recorded but probably refers to Chicheley Hall (HE: 1000596), Chicheley, Buckinghamshire, home of the Chester family. Notable amongst them was Sir Anthony Chester (1566-1635), who was created Baronet of Chicheley (1620) upon the favour of George Villiers, Duke of Buckingham (1616-28), himself favourite of King James I (Waters 1878: 112). He was succeeded by his son (1593-1652) and grandson (1633-98) of the same name (HoP). The meaning of '*m' Come buck*' is unclear, but 'come' may refer to the *comitem* tile of the Chesters, with 'buck' being a reference to Buckinghamshire.

This vervel was found close to a silver bell (NMS-2C2226), perhaps associated with hawking, though another use is possible. Although the findspot is some distance away from the Chicheley family home (over 100km), there is another connection between the Chicheleys and Emneth. Elizabeth and Dorothy Peynton, daughters of John Peyton, married into families associated with both places. Elizabeth married Anthony Chester (later 2nd baronet) in 1623, and Dorothy married Lawrence Oxburgh of Emneth; it was at Hackbeach Hall – seemingly destroyed, but perhaps close to Hagbeach House (HE: 1077702) – that John Peyton died in 1658 (Waters 1878: 315-8), the house coming into the possession of the Peyntons by 1628 (Chambers 1829:

485). The vervel was found about 2km south of the main hamlet of Emneth, and the site of its manor-house.

Location: Norwich Castle Museum.

M Lewis, S Ashley & E Darch

Vervel from Emneth (NMS-2C1204) (courtesy of the Portable Antiquities Scheme).

A20 NORFOLK, FRANSHAM (NMS-092867; 2009 T532)

Date: c.1600-c.1684.

Description: Silver flat circular ring, rectangular in section, inscribed on both faces in capital letters in Latin script: W. SPRYNG / OF PAKENHAM. 12mm x 1mm. 0.64g.

Discussion: This vervel is likely to be associated with a member of the Spring family who resided at Packenham Hall (now demolished), Suffolk; their seat between 1545 and 1735. During the 17th century Sir William Spring (1588-1638), who served as High Sheriff of Suffolk (in 1596 and 1621), was knighted (1610), and served as Member of Parliament (for Suffolk and Bury St Edmunds) at various times between 1624 and 1629 (HoP). His son, also called William (1613-54), was created baronet (1642) by King Charles I, even though he was a Parliamentarian. Like his father he served as High Sheriff (1641) and was Member of Parliament for Suffolk (elected in 1679 and 1681) (HoP). It is likely that this vervel is associated with one of these two men. William (the younger) was succeeded by his son, Thomas (d. 1704).

Pakenham is some 55km south of Fransham, where this vervel was found. About 900m from the findspot is Dunham Lodge (HE: 1077493), a late 18th century mansion, and 1800m away is the Old Manor (HE: 1152599) of Little Fransham. Also at Great Fransham, some 1200m away, is the site of a medieval manor (Norfolk HER: 24783). It is possible that the Spring family had an association with local gentry in the vicinity, explaining the vervel's loss here.

Location: Norwich Castle Museum.

I Richardson, E Darch & M Lewis

Vervel from Fransham (NMS-092867) (courtesy of the Portable Antiquities Scheme).

A21 NORFOLK, WYMONDHAM (NMS-A8D4D7; 2011 T715)

Date: c.1593-c.1608.

Description: Silver flat circular ring, rectangular in section, inscribed on both faces in capital letters in Latin script: {cross} HENRYE CLARE / OF STANFELD. Slightly buckled. 14.5mm x 1mm. 1.15g.

Discussion: Henry Clare (Clere) lived at Stanfield Hall between 24 June 1593 and 1608. Little is known about this individual, apart from that in 1608 he benefited from the acquisition of new lands in Ireland, in the Precinct of Liffer (O'Laughlin 2001: 12); by 1610 these lands incorporated 450 acres around Shraghnurlar, held in demesne with 'a court baron' for 8 English shillings (Hill 2004: 271).

The extant Stanfield Hall (HE: 119672) was built in 1792, altered in 1830-5, but includes earlier fabric, some dating to the 16th century; Stanfield Hall is set within a medieval moated site, on the site of a medieval manor (Norfolk HER: 9457). The vervel was found 900m from the manor site, some 2km south-east of Wymondham.

Location: Norwich Castle Museum.

M Lewis & A Marsden

Vervel from Wymondham (NMS-A8D4D7) (courtesy of the Portable Antiquities Scheme).

A22 NORTHAMPTONSHIRE, BARNWELL (BH-64FD13; 2015 T789)

Date: c.1580-c.1684.

Description: Silver flat circular ring, rectangular in section, inscribed on one face in italic script: *{six-pointed star} Edw. Lord. Mountague.* 11.4mm x 1mm. 0.56g.

Description: It is likely that the inscription refers to Edward Montagu (1563-1644), who was a Member of Parliament (1584-1621), for various constituencies: Bere Alston 1584-5, Tavistock 1597-8, Brackley 1601-4, Northamptonshire 1604-21), before being ennobled on 29 June 1621 as the 1st Baron Montagu of Boughton, Northamptonshire. He sponsored the Observance of the 5th November Act 1605, but his royalist sympathies saw him arrested during the English Civil War (in 1642), perishing as a prisoner two years later at the Savoy Hospital. His son (by his second marriage, to Frances Cotton), also named Edward, was a Member of Parliament for Huntington (from 1640) until the death of his father (1644), when he was elected to the House of Lords. He served Charles I, Cromwell and Charles II, and was a royalist at heart; in 1647 Charles I visited to play bowls at Boughton while under arrest. After the Restoration (1662), Lord Edward mostly resided at Boughton Hall, were he died in 1684. It is likely that this vervel is associated with the hawking activities of one of these two men.

Boughton Hall and its gardens (HE: 1000375) were substantially redeveloped in the late 17th and early 18th centuries. However, this ancestral home of the Montagu family is some 17km west of the vervel's findspot. Closer is Barnwell Castle (HE: 1294426), which is of medieval date. Intriguingly this castle, which is only 2km from the findspot, came into the possession of Sir Edmund Montagu in 1540, and by 1586 it is know the place was 'repaired and beautified with new buildings' (ibid.). Close by the Montagu's built Barnwell Manor (HE: 1040281), probably from the late 16th century.

Location: Returned to finder/landowner.

J Watters, M Lewis & I Richardson

Vervel from Barnwell (BH-64FD13) (courtesy of the Portable Antiquities Scheme).

A23 SOMERSET, CHURCHSTANTON (SOM-AD9013; 2009 T667)

Date: c.1600-c.1646.

Description: Silver flat circular ring, rectangular in section, inscribed on one face in italic script: *{eight-pointed star} Cothelstoe in Somerset.* 12.22mm x 0.96mm.

Discussion: The vervel was found attached to a large gold loop, along with a small lump of iron and a gold-plated disc with foliate design. It has been postulated that all the objects might be associated with hawking (Paul Manning, *pers. comm.*), although the gold-plated disc is almost certainly the remains of an 18th or 19th century pocket watch winder, and as such it seems likely that the group was collated as trinkets by an unknown person, well after the time when the vervel was in use.

The vervel is not inscribed with a personal name, but it is almost certainly associated with Cothelstone manor (HE: 1001141), located about 18km north of the findspot. This house was originally built in the mid-16th century, before being largely destroyed by canon fire in 1646, after its owners, the Stawell's (Stowell) sided with the Royalists during the English Civil War. Although the estate was handed back to the family after the Restoration the house was not rebuilt until 1855-6. It seems likely, therefore, that this vervel belonged to a hawk owned by Sir John Stawell (1600-62), or maybe his father of the same name. John (the younger) was MP for Somerset, first in 1625, during the Long Parliament of 1640-2, and after the Restoration until his death (1661-2); he was imprisoned for the whole of the Commonweath period on charges of high reason, but the case was never settled (HoP). At the church of St Thomas 'of Canterbury' at Cothelstone is an impressive alabaster tomb to Sir John (d.1603) and his wife, Frances Dyer.

Location: Returned to finder/landowner.

A Booth, G Egan & M Lewis

Vervel from Churchstanton (SOM-AD9013) – detail (courtesy of the Portable Antiquities Scheme).

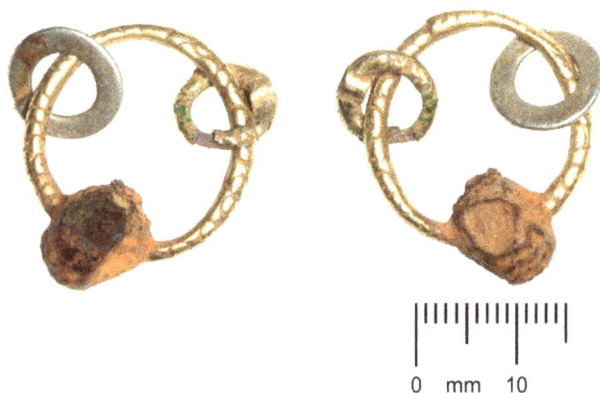

Gold loop, attached with vervel and other objects (courtesy of the Portable Antiquities Scheme).

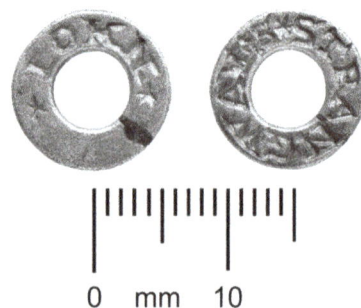

Vervel from East Chinnock (SOM-E93B19) (courtesy of the Portable Antiquities Scheme).

A24 SOMERSET, EAST CHINNOCK (SOM-E93B19; 2017 T533)

Date: c.1600-1666.

Description: Silver flat circular ring, rectangular in section, inscribed on both faces in capital letters: *{six-pointed star}* IOHN *{six-pointed star}* / *{six-pointed star}* STRANGWAYES. 12mm x 5.4mm x 1.3mm. 0.87g. A small black line, perpendicular to the circumference and extending between the external and internal edges, possibly of a tarnished less pure silver, appears to be a repair.

Discussion: The vervel appears to name John Strangways 'of Melbury Sampford' (1583-1666), who served as an MP for both the 'Dorset' and 'Weymouth and Melcombe Regis' constituencies at various points between 1614 and 1666; in Parliament he was noted as 'a potent opponent' and 'a wise, crafty and experienced man' (HoP). During the English Civil War he sided with the Royalists and was imprisoned afterwards (1645-8), thereafter caused no trouble during the Interregnum, but welcomed the Restoration. The Strangways were based at Melbury House (HE: 1119248), originally built for Giles Strangway in c.1530, but rebuilt and extended in the 17th, 18th and 19th centuries; this estate is some 10km south-east of the findspot.

In the vicinity of the findspot are some 17th century listed buildings including Manor Farmhouse at Middle Chinnock (HE: 1057127), to the west, and Weston House at East Chinnock (HE: 1057208), in the east; the latter dates to 1637. An exact connection between John Strangways and the findspot has not been found, but it is known that Sir John gifted to the poor of the parishes of Middle and West Chinnock in 1664 (HoC 1827: 371), hence suggesting a local connection which might also explain a hawking venture (and therefore the loss of the vervel) in the area.

Location: Museum of Somerset.

L Burnett, W Partridge & I Richardson

A25 STAFFORDSHIRE, ALREWAS & FRADLEY (NARC-7CF046; 2010 T137)

Date: c.1600-c.1700.

Description: Silver flat circular ring, rectangular in section, inscribed on both faces in italic script: *Tho: Wigley of / Midlton*. 14mm.

Discussion: The place named on this vervel probably refers to Middleton-by-Wirksworth, Derbyshire, though almost 50km north-east of the findspot. Here resided, in 'the Gatehouse' (HE: 1109609) – which is likely to be upon the site on an earlier structure – Thomas Wigley, eldest son of Henry Wigley (d.1610). It is perhaps he who died on 17 February 1635 (NA: PROB 11/167/192) without issue, although another Thomas Wigley (presumably related) became a Freeman of the borough of Derby in 1648 (Wigley 1965: 582); the genealogy and history of the family is sketchy not least because of the commonality of certain first names, including Henry and Thomas. Indeed, by 1666 a certain Thomas 'of Wirksworth' was issuing trade tokens displaying the arms of the grocers' company (Hackett 1899: 169).

About 300m from where this vervel was found is Orgeave Hall (HE: 1374275), the original house being built in c.1668 (for the manor). The manor of Alrewas came into the possession of John Turton and his brother, Philip, after purchasing it for £3130 on 3 January 1660 (Pitt 1817: 65); John, who was knighted and became a Justice of the Court of the Kings Bench at Westminster, died in 1708 (NA: PROB 11/500/239). To date, no other link has been found between the Wigley's and Orgeave Hall, though it seems likely the former had been invited to hunt there in the late 17th century. From 1752 Orgeave Hall passed to the Viscounts Anson, later earls of Litchfield.

Location: Returned to finder/landowner.

M Lewis, T Brindle & D Thornton

Vervel from Alrewas & Fradley (NARC-7CF046) (courtesy of the Portable Antiquities Scheme).

A26 WARWICKSHIRE, BILLESLEY (PAS-B05027; 2010 T788)

Date: c.1608-c.1659.

Description: Silver flat circular ring, rectangular in section, inscribed on both faces in italic script: *{six-pointed star} Sr Robert Lee / of Bilseley*; long tail on letters 'R' and end 'e' in 'Lee'. 12mm x 0.5mm. 0.45g.

Discussion: This vervel is likely to be associated with one of three generations of the Lee (Leigh) family who resided at Billesley Manor, Warwickshire (HE: 1382696; Warwickshire CR: MWA3695), and was found in close proximity to the manor house. In 1600 the manor was sold to Sir Robert Lee (d.1605), a London merchant and one-time Mayor of London for £5,000 (BHO). This Robert Lee, settled the manor upon his son, also Robert (knighted in 1608), and his wife, Ann. It was under this Sir Robert that, between 1610 and 1620, work began rebuilding the manor in stone. This Robert Lee (II), had a son of the same name (c.1602-59), who succeeded him in 1637. Sir Robert Lee (III) died with no male issue, leaving the manor to his daughter, Anne, who sold it off (ibid). It is likely, therefore, that this vervel belonged to a hawk associated with either of the last two Sir Robert's.

Location: Warwickshire Museum; donated by finder/landowner, with a seal matrix identified with Robert Lee (III) found nearby.

I Richardson & M Lewis

Vervel from Billesley (PAS-B05027) (courtesy of the Portable Antiquities Scheme).

Seal matrix of Sir Robert Lee (III), made during the lifetime of his father (WAW-5EF2D8) (courtesy of the Portable Antiquities Scheme).

A27 WARWICKSHIRE, BILLESLEY (WAW-585A60; 2017 T1023)

Date: c.1610-c.1637.

Description: Silver flat circular ring, rectangular in section, inscribed on one face in italic script: *{six-pointed star} Robert. Lee {cross} Esqr. / {blank}*. 13.14mm x 1.12mm. 0.82g.

Discussion: This vervel was found about 50m away from the vervel above (**A26**) and is also associated with the Lee family. The finder has conjected that this (given it is inscribed esquire) might have been for a bird owned by the youngest Robert Lee (III) (c.1602-59), presumably before his father died in 1637.

Location: Warwickshire Museum; donated by finder/landowner.

A Bolton & M Lewis

Vervel from Billesley (WAW-585A60) (courtesy of the Portable Antiquities Scheme).

A28 WARWICKSHIRE, WELLESBOURNE
(PAS-2BC222; 2005 T257)

Date: c.1600-c.1640.

Description: Silver flat circular ring, rectangular in section, inscribed on both faces in italic script: {*eight-pointed star*} *Sr Thomas Luci / of Charlecote* {*eight-pointed star*}. 10mm x 1mm. 0.58g.

Discussion: The Lucy family were important local aristocrats whose descendants held the manor of Charlecote since at least 1189 (BHO; HE: 1001187), a little over 2km from the findspot. By 1558 the old manor was replaced with the current building (HE: 1381799) by Sir Thomas Lucy (1532-1600), best known as a fervent Protestant who arrested and interrogated local Catholics, including members of the Arden family, relatives of William Shakespeare; Shakespeare himself, purportedly, poached from the Charlecote estate (Bate & Thornton 2012: 66-7). Both Sir Lucy's son (d. 1605) and grandson (1585-1640) were also named Thomas. Little is recorded of Thomas (II), but it is known that as sheriff of Warwickshire he was reprimanded by the Privy Council whilst in office for attempting to manipulate the 1601 Warwickshire parliamentary election (HoP); won by Fulke Greville and Sir Robert Digby. Thomas (III) inherited from his father aged 19, and had an adventurous youth, being sent home from France by the English ambassador in 1609 for his 'propensity for dueling', becoming shipwrecked near Dover, and noted for his collection of books. He was MP for Warwickshire from 1614 until 1629 (when Parliament was suspended by Charles II), and then for Warwick in 1640, but died later that year. It is likely that either of these two men (Thomas II or III) once owned the hawk associated with this vervel.

Location: Warwickshire Museum.

S Wear, M Lewis & I Richardson

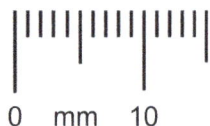

Vervel from Wellesbourne (PAS-2BC222) (courtesy of the Portable Antiquities Scheme).

William Shakespeare standing before Sir Thomas Lucy (sitting at right) after poaching a deer, engraving in the British Museum (©The Trustees of the British Museum).

A29 WILTSHIRE, WEST LAVINGTON (WILT-F4C291; 2017 T1041)

Date: c.1600-c.1700.

Description: Silver flat circular ring, rectangular in section, inscribed on one face in italic script: *West Lavington Wilts*. 12.37mm x 1mm. 0.67g.

Discussion: This vervel was found in the place that it mentions, and close to West Lavington Manor (HE: 1035895), of which parts of the extant building date to the 16th century. The vervel does not give the name of the bird's owner, but by 1630 West Lavington (formerly Bishop's Lavington) Manor was owned and occupied by Sir John Dauntsey (c.1555-1630), and the porch of the manor house has the initials of the Dauntseys. This family had owned land in the area from as early as 1474, and thereafter the manor was occupied by relatives of the Dauntseys, the Danvers, and their descendants as tenants (BHO). It seems likely, therefore, the vervel is associated with one of these families, quite likely the Dauntseys, perhaps Sir John himself.

Location: Returned to finder/landowner.

J Hanbidge, I Richardson & M Lewis

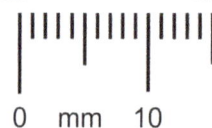

Vervel from West Lavington (WILT-F4C291) (courtesy of the Portable Antiquities Scheme).

A30 YORKSHIRE (NORTH), DALTON
(NCL-9FC501; 2006 T590)

Date: c.1400-c.1500.

Description: Silver flat circular ring, rectangular in section, inscribed on one face in italic script: + + I + II + I + I + + / ure *{sprigs of foliage}* ?v *{sprigs of foliage}*. 16mm.

Discussion: The inscription upon this vervel appears to be nonsensical, though 'ure' might represent a place-name; it is not clear whether the 'v' is a letter or just part of the plant motif. The form of the script, however, suggests a later medieval date. The vervel was found in the immediate vicinity of Dalton Hall (HE: 1131349), a fortified manor house which dates back to the 15th century, and was modified in the late 16th or early 17th century, and more recently also.

Dalton is a township within the ancient parish of Kirby Ravensworth, and by the late 13th century there were three Daltons in the parish, which complicates understanding the history of the parish. In the early 14th century the manor (Dalton Ryall) was sold to Sir Nicholas Stapleton (1280-1343), and it seems (more or less) to have stayed in that family until it passed (in 1373-4) to the Methams of Metham (East Yorkshire). This family still had the manor in 1539 (BHO), and therefore are most likely to be associated with the vervel described above.

Location: Returned to finder/landowner.

M Lewis & R Collins

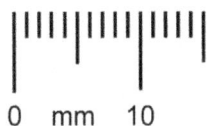

Vervel from Dalton (NCL-9FC501) (courtesy of the Portable Antiquities Scheme).

A31 YORKSHIRE (NORTH), KNARESBOROUGH
(SWYOR-9CBF24; 2012 T613)

Date: c.1600-c.1642.

Description: Silver flat circular ring, rectangular in section, inscribed on both faces in italic script: *{eight-pointed star} Sir William* / *{eight-pointed star x 3} Sheffeild.* 11.79mm x 1.38mm. 0.74g.

Discussion: The person named on this vervel is probably Sir William Sheffield of Mowthorpe (1589/90-1646), one

of the MPs for Hedon-in-Holderness (1614-21) and Thirsk (1624-5). Records show that he was not particularly active in Parliament, and he left England for the Low Countries on the advent of the English Civil War settling amongst the English community in Delft (HoP). There is a memorial to him and his first wife, Elizabeth (married in 1615), in the church of St Martin le Grand, York.

The vervel was found less than 1km from Goldsborough Hall (HE: 1315586), built for Sir Richard Hutton (1560-1639) between 1601 and 1625. His son, of the same name (1617-45), was MP for Knaresborough (1621-9) and was killed at the Battle of Sherburn-in-Elmet on 15 October 1645 while serving the King (HoP). Although the two men (Sheffield and Hutton) were in Parliament at the same time (including 1624-5), such as during a debate on breaking the treaty with Spain in 1624, their potential association is unknown, and politically unlikely from 1642. Perhaps then it was during the earlier part of the 17th century that the vervel bearing Sheffeld's name was lost near Hutton's family seat.

Location: Harrogate Museum.

M Lewis & A Downes

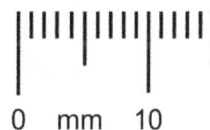

Vervel from Knaresborough (SWYOR-9CBF24) (courtesy of the Portable Antiquities Scheme).

A32 YORKSHIRE (NORTH), MELSONBY
(DUR-756E12; 2010 T825)

Date: c.1600-c.1700.

Description: Silver flat circular ring, rectangular in section, inscribed on both faces in italic script: *Witt {eight-pointed star} Shawa {eight-pointed star, six-pointed star}* / *{eight-pointed star x 3} of {eight-pointed star} Melsemby* [?a]. 13.33mm x 1.02mm. 0.9g.

Discussion: The name inscribed upon this vervel is unclear, though it is apparent that Melsemby probably stands for Melsonby. At the beginning of the 17th century the manor of Melsonby was in the hands of the Gowers, who in 1623 settled it on Solomon Wyvill, and his heirs, and John Robinson. None of these families seem to be named on the vervel.

Some buildings in the eastern part of Melsonby, and therefore closest to the findspot (some just 400m away), date to the 17th century. These include The Old Rectory

(HE: 1131888), but (again) associations between these places and the vervel are unclear.

Location: Returned to finder/landowner.

F McIntosh & M Lewis

Vervel from Melsonby (DUR-756E12) (courtesy of the Portable Antiquities Scheme).

Vervel from Middleton (DUR-A20CB7) (courtesy of the Portable Antiquities Scheme).

A33 YORKSHIRE (NORTH), MIDDLETON
(DUR-A20CB7; 2014 T535)

Date: c.1650-c.1705.

Description: Silver flat circular ring, sub-rectangular in section, inscribed on one face in italic script: *M: Watkinson Payler*. 13.11mm x 0.88mm. 0.8g.

Discussion: This vervel almost certainly belonged to a hunting bird of Sir Watkinson Payler (c.1634-1705) of Thoralby, and son of Sir Edward Payler (created 1st Baronet in 1642) and Anne Watkinson; there is a memorial to Sir Edward in the Church of St Andrew, Bugthorpe, East Yorkshire (HE: 1309966). The family seat of the Paylers was nearby Thoralby Hall (demolished, but earthworks visible), now replaced by newer farm buildings (Thoralby Hall Farm), north-west of the church. Watkinson Payler succeeded his father to as Baronet of Thoralby in 1647, but died without issue (Burke & Burke 1841: 404). He was one of the MPs for Malton (1679-85), though he does not seem to have been particularly active in Parliament (HoP).

Although the vervel findspot is some 32km north of Thoralby, it is much closer to Sir Watkinson Payler's parliamentary seat of Malton (some 16km away). At Middleton there are some 17th century buildings, such as Church Farmhouse (HE: 1149719), but it is not clear which of these (if any) might have a connection with a visitation of Watkinson Payler.

Location: Returned to finder/landowner.

M Lewis, E Cox & L Proctor

Wales

A34 VALE OF GLAMORGAN, LLANTRITHYD
(PAS-B5EC63; 2001 W7)

Date: c.1620-1641.

Description: Silver flat circular ring, rectangular in section, inscribed on one face in italic script: *{six-pointed star} John. Awbrey. Esqr.* 11.5mm. 0.64g.

Discussion: This vervel is almost certainly associated with the Aubrey family of Breconshire, who had acquired land and wealth thanks to Dr William Aubrey (c.1529-95) being in high favour with Elizabeth I; it is said by the antiquarian John Aubrey (William's great grandson) that the Queen was so fond of him she called him 'her little doctor' (DNB). Nothing of this was left to William Aubrey's second son, Sir Thomas (1565-1641), who was already well provided for through his marriage (in 1586) to Mary, elder daughter and co-heiress of Anthony Mansel of Llantrithyd. Thomas was the first Aubrey to come to Llantrithyd, where he lived at Llantrithyd Place (CADW: 13594), the ancestral home of his mother-in-law, Elizabeth Bassett; the vervel was found only 130m from the now ruined manor house.

When Sir Thomas died, Llantrithyd was left to his eldest son, John (1605-79), the individual that appears to be named on the vervel; since John is here titled esquire, it might be presumed his father was still living when the object was made. John Aubrey was a staunch royalist, who was active in the Royalist rising in Glamorgan in 1646. He styled himself Sir John from 1644, when a warrant was issued for him to be made a baronet; this was not sealed until the Restoration. During the English Civil War, Llantrithyd was sequestered by Parliament, but Sir John recovered it in 1650 thereafter making it a refuge for Royalist academics and clergymen.

Location: Returned to finder/landowner.

M Lewis & M Redknap

A35 WREXHAM, BRONINGTON (HESH-C74F57; 2011 W12)

Date: c.1600-c.1700.

Description: Silver flat circular ring, rectangular in section, inscribed on one face in italic script: *{five-pointed star} Somerford Co. Chester. Esq.* The metallic composition of this vervel has been scientifically tested, showing it to be approximately 96% silver and 4% copper. 11.6mm x 0.75mm. 0.7g.

Discussion: The manor of Somerford, Cheshire, is recorded in the Domesday Book, and was held by a family of that name until the late 16th century, when the male line expired. The estates subsequently passed between prominent local gentry, including the Bridges, Oldfields and Shakerleys, and the vervel probably belonged to a hawk of one of these families.

Why this vervel came to be lost in Bronington is unclear. There are 17th century buildings in the general vicinity of the findspot, such as Maesllwyn House (CADW: 1654) and New Hall Farm (CADW: 85478), but none known to be associated with Somerton or the families from there.

Location: Wrexham Museum.

S Iles, M Redknap, Z Burford, M Lewis & P Reavill

Vervel from Wrexham (HESH-C74F57) (courtesy of the Portable Antiquities Scheme).

Type B (Ring) Vervels

England

B01 BERKSHIRE, ALDERMASTON (BH-0FB1A8; 2015 T342)

Date: c.1630-c.1711.

Description: Silver ring, circular in plan (now distorted), and D-shaped in section. Its exterior face is inscribed in italic script: *of Aldermaston com {?} barks*; the word Aldermaston features a long (or medial) letter s. There is a break of approximately 1mm, where the two ends of the ring joined, just at the letter n. 9.2mm x 2.85mm. 0.3g

Discussion: The inscription marks the vervel as belonging to a hunting bird of an owner from Aldermaston in the county of Berkshire. The findspot is in the vicinity of the 19th century Aldermaston Court (HE: 1117317), the successor to Aldermaston House; the original house was completed in 1636 by Sir Humphrey Forster (1595-1663), 1st Baronet Aldermaston, and his wife, Anne. Sir Humphrey was a loyalist during the English Civil War, which saw some conflict between the two sides on the grounds of the estate.

Sir Humphrey and Anne had many children, but few survived to adulthood. His second son, William, died in 1661 and it was his son (Sir Humphrey's grandson), another Sir Humphrey (1650-1711), who succeeded to the baronetcy, and became a member of Parliament for Berkshire (HoP). Judging from the style of the inscription, it seems plausible that this vervel belonged to the 1st Baronet or one of his children or grandchildren.

Location: West Berkshire Museum.

I Richardson & J Watters

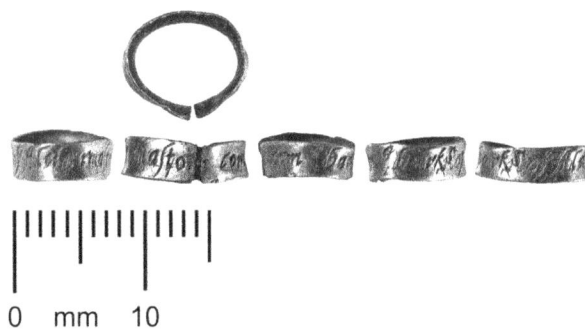

Vervel from Aldermaston (BH-0FB1A8) (courtesy of the Portable Antiquities Scheme).

B02 DORSET, HORTON (DOR-62DF93; 2012 T793)

Date: c.1700-c.1786.

Description: Silver ring, circular in plan and D-shaped in section; the edges are irregular and show signs of use or damage. Its outer face is crudely inscribed in serifed letters on the exterior of the band: H=S at Horton, Dorset. 2.45mm x 9.01mm. 0.5g.

Discussion: The initials on this vervel may refer to a member of the local Sturt family. Humphrey Sturt (1687-1740), son of Sir Anthony Sturt (c.1656-1741), married Diana Napier (d.1740) in 1718/19. Their son, another Humphrey Sturt (c.1724-86), was five-times an MP for Dorsetshire and was responsible for the construction (in 1742) of a local folly, the six-story Horton Tower, which survives to this day (HE: 1120082). In 1765 Humphrey Sturt inherited the Crichel Estate through his mother's side of the family, and moved the family seat to Crichel House (HE: 1120155), 3km distant from the vervel findspot (Robinson 2017). Horton Manor, the original Sturt family home, was closer to the village, and nearby to the findspot. It deteriorated soon after the move to Crichel House and was demolished sometime after (Conservation Areas in East Dorset 2006).

The potential 18th-century date of this vervel would make it one of the later examples reported as Treasure via the Portable Antiquities Scheme, indicating use of this object beyond the period of falconry's apogee. If attributed to the latter Humphrey Sturt, this adds weight to the story that he supposedly used Horton Tower as a platform from which to observe the hunt; the vervel was found about 1km from the Tower.

Location: Priest's House Museum, Wimborne.

C Hayward-Trevarthen & I Richardson

Vervel from Horton (DOR-62DF93) (courtesy of the Portable Antiquities Scheme).

Horton Tower (©Mike Searle).

B03 DORSET, PUDDLETOWN (DOR-B83652; 2007 T168)

Date: c.1600-c.1700.

Description: Silver ring, circular in plan and D-shaped in section. It is inscribed on its outer face in italic script: {cross potent} *At mounckton in dorsett*. No dimensions recorded.

Discussion: Mounckton is the contemporary equivalent of Monkton, of which there are three places bearing this name in Dorset: Monkton Wyld, Tarrant Monkton and Winterbourne Monkton. Winterborne Monkton is closest to the findspot, and one source cites the name 'Mounckton' as a predecessor to the current parish name (Pentin 1906). Though this parish itself seems to lack a major landholder, neighbouring Winterborne Herringston is home to the 16th century Herringston House (HE: 1119179), owned since 1513 by the Williams family (BHO). The house was extensively remodelled by Sir John Williams (1545-1617), MP for Dorset in 1604 (HoP), who was succeeded by his grandson, another John Williams, whose dates are not recorded (Burke & Burke 1847: 1593).

The findspot is roughly 2km to the east of Waterston Manor (HE: 1119080), which in 1641 passed to John Strangways (1585-1666), who has been identified as the likely owner of **A24**, above.

Location: Returned to finder/landowner.

I Richardson & D Thornton

Vervel from Puddletown (DOR-B83652) (courtesy of the Portable Antiquities Scheme).

B04 ESSEX, LAYER-DE-LA-HAYE (ESS-728703; 2014 T174)

Date: c.1600-c.1700.

Description: Silver ring, circular in plan and roughly D-shaped in section; the outer face is flat and inscribed in italic script: {six-pointed star} *Layer de la haye. in. Essex.* 9.3mm. 0.67g.

Discussion: The inscription indicates that the owner of the bird which lost this vervel resided in Layer-de-la-Haye. The vervel was found very close to the site of the former Layer Hall (not listed), seat of the Manor of Layer-de-la-Haye, which in the 16th century was occupied by the Tey family who had owned the manor for almost 200 years. In 1594, Thomas Tey (dates unknown) sold the manor to Peter Bettenson (dates unknown), and the Bettenson family maintained residence there until 1734 (Hopkirk 1934: 4-8). Perhaps the most prominent member of the family residing in Layer during the 17th century was Sir Richard Bettenson, (c.1601-79); he was the last person knighted by King James I, at Royston in 1625 (Nichols 1828: 1028).

Location: Colchester & Ipswich Museums Service.

I Richardson & K Marsden

Vervel from Layer-de-la-Haye (ESS-728703) (courtesy of the Portable Antiquities Scheme).

B05 ESSEX, TOPPLESFIELD area (ESS-BE1B12; 2011 T309)

Date: c.1600-c.1700.

Description: Silver ring, circular in plan, and D-shaped in section. The outer face of the ring is flat and inscribed in italic script: *Iohn Stepkin of.* 8.84mm x 2.51mm x 1.35mm. 0.6g.

Discussion: This vervel is presumably one of a pair, of which the other would have named the place of residence of the owner, John Stepkin. The Essex Record Office (D/ABW 46/238) contains the will of a John Stepkin of Great Leighs, who resided 15 miles south of the findspot. He died in 1624, and left a son also named John Stepkin, but any connection with either of them is conjecture.

The findspot is in close proximity to Cust Hall (HE: 1317406) a house whose core dates to the early 16th century. In the 17th century it is attributed to the Crachrode family (Metcalfe 1878). 600m from the findspot is the moated site of Berwick Hall (HE: 1122992), a house of early 17th century (in fact dated on a gable 1635) but altered later (BHO). No further details on who resided there in the 17th century, or any association with John Stepkin, have been discovered, but it seems likely they are somehow connected.

Location: Returned to finder/landowner.

L McLean, I Richardson & M Lewis

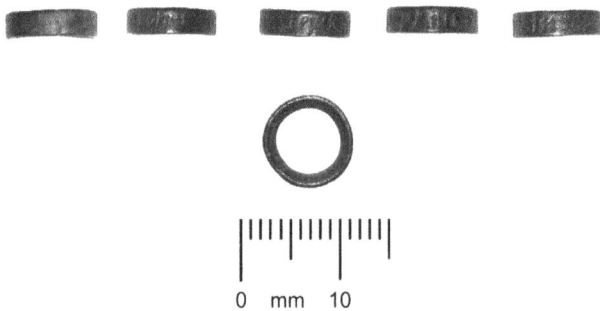

Vervel from Topplesfield area (ESS-BE1B12) (courtesy of the Portable Antiquities Scheme).

B06 HAMPSHIRE, MICHELDEVER (SUR-02A7B4; 2012 T347)

Date: c.1575-c.1625.

Description: Silver ring, circular in plan, and D-shaped in section. The outer face of the ring is flat, inscribed in italics: {six-pointed star} *Sr.Hen.Browne.of* (or possibly 'Hon' rather than 'Hen'). 9.86 mm x 2.84 mm. 0.59g

Discussion: The vervel was found in the Stratton Park area of Micheldever, in the same vicinity as **A11**, **A12** and **B07**, as a group dated between c.1575 and c.1683. The latter (**B07**) was found nearby (see below), is similar in size, weight and style, and has the complimentary inscription – *{six-pointed star} Stratton. in. Hampshrie.*

The Sir Henry Browne, to whose hawk this vervel was once attached, appears to be named in the Journal of the House of Lords from 1 May 1645 which 'ORDERED, That Mrs Frances Burby and Mrs Eliz. Newell, with Anthony Tingle and Ric'd Browninge, their Two Men, shall have a Pass, to come from *Sir Henry Browne*'s House in East Stratton, Hampshire, to London' (BHO).

Other references to this Sir Henry Browne are difficult to trace. It is possible that he was a relative of Anthony Browne, 1st Viscount Montagu (1528-92), especially if the inscription reads 'Hon.' (for Honourable) – a courtesy title applied to the sons of the nobility. Anthony Browne's third son, and second by his second wife Magdalen Dacre (d.1608), was Sir Henry Browne (born after 1558).

The Browne family owned Cowdray House, Midhurst, West Sussex (HE: 1001210), and Sir Henry is known to have organised the hunting events for Queen Elizabeth I and her retinue during her six-day visit to Cowdray in 1591 (Adams 2012: 155). Another Henry Browne with whom this vervel might be associated was the 5th Viscount Montagu (1640-1717) though this would appear to be someone other than the Henry Browne referenced in the House of Lords Journal.

Stratton Park (HE: 1000867) itself was owned during 17th century by Thomas Wrothesley, 4th Earl of Southampton (1607-67) and passed to his daughter, Lady Rachel (c.1636-1723), wife of William Lord Russell (1639-83), who is associated with **A11**. Perhaps then, Sir Henry attended a hunting party on the Earl of Southampton's land.

Location: Returned to finder/landowner.

I Richardson & D Williams

Vervel from Micheldever (SUR-02A7B4) (courtesy of the Portable Antiquities Scheme).

Cowdray House in Ruins, watercolour by Charles Wild (© The Trustees of the British Museum).

B07 HAMPSHIRE, MICHELDEVER (PUBLIC-AD2F70; 2015 T442)

Date: c.1575-c.1625.

Description: Silver ring, circular in plan, and D-shaped in section. Its flat external face is inscribed in italic script: *{six-pointed star} Stratton. in. Hampshrie.* 9.36 mm x 2.64 mm x 1.21 mm. 0.58g

Discussion: This vervel is of almost identical diameter and weight to **B06** (as already described) and was found approximately 900m away from it. It is possible, though only speculative, that they once adorned the same bird, or two different birds flown by the same owner.

Location: Returned to finder/landowner; subsequently sold at auction (Bonhams 19/1/17: Lot 60).

I Richardson & C Hayward-Trevarthern

Vervel from Micheldever (PUBLIC-AD2F70) (courtesy of the Portable Antiquities Scheme).

Stratton Park in Hampshire, engraving in the British Library (courtesy of the British Library Mechanical Curator Collection).

B08 HAMPSHIRE, THRUXTON (HAMP-AA8A10; 2011 T370)

Date: c.1600-c.1634.

Description: Silver ring, sub-circular in plan, and D-shaped in section. The top and bottom edges are dented. The exterior of the band is flat, but worn, and inscribed in italics: *{six-pointed star} Sr John Philpott of.* 9.7mm x 8.55mm x 2.8mm. 0.61g.

Discussion: This vervel is likely to have belonged to a hunting bird owned by John Philpot (1576-1634), who was lord of the manor of Thruxton between 1624 and 1634, but who (along with his wife and children) was

declared a papist in 1624 (Anonymous: 1751; 326) and had the property confiscated (BHO).

The vervel was found approximately 1km from the site of a fortified manor (HE: 1001871), and associated manor house (HE: 1093205), which was rebuilt in the 18th century.

Location: Hampshire Cultural Trust.

E Vandyk, R Webley & I Richardson

Vervel from Thruxton (HAMP-AA8A10) (courtesy of the Portable Antiquities Scheme).

B09 HERTFORDSHIRE, BALDOCK area (BH-01EC33; 2007 T24)

Date: c.1600-c.1630.

Description: Silver ring, sub-circular in plan, and D-shaped in section. The exterior of the ring is flat and engraved: *{six-pointed star} Sr. Edmond.Lucye.* The letters E and the L are straight serifed Roman initials, while the others are italicised. 9mm x 2.6mm. 0.67g.

Discussion: In 1622, a Sir Edmond Lucy (died c.1630) held the manor at Ponsbourne, near Hatfield (now the site of a 19th century hotel, with no 17th century buildings surviving); this is approximately 30km south of the findspot. Edmond Lucy owned Ponsbourne by virtue of his wife, daughter of the previous owner, Henry Cock (dates unknown) of Broxbourne. One source reports that Sir Edmond was married to Elizabeth Cock (BHO), however a monument in the parish church of St Augustine's, Broxbourne, relates that his wife was a different daughter of Henry Cock, named Frances (Chauncey 1826: 570).

The closest notable building to the findspot itself is Bygrave Manor House (HE: 1102685), less than 1km away. This was owned in the late 16th century by William Warren *alias* Bygrave (died 1588-9). His son, another William (dates unknown), sold the manor in 1613 to William Whettell (dates unknown) of Thetford and Sir John Heveningham (1577-1633) of Ketteringham, Norfolk; the latter assumed sole ownership. Sir John's son, William Heveningham (dates unknown), in turn sold the manor to Francis Cleaver (dates unknown) in 1651, and Cleaver's son Charles (dates unknown) sold it to James, the 3rd Earl of Salisbury (1648-83), in 1682 (BHO). It may be, therefore, that William Whettel or (more likely) Sir John Heveningham were entertaining Sir Edmond Lucy when this vervel was lost, but no records placing them together have been found.

Location: Returned to finder/landowner.

I Richardson, J Watters, & D Thornton

Vervel from Baldock area (BH-01EC33) (courtesy of the Portable Antiquities Scheme).

B10 KENT, BADLESMERE (KENT-8DE94E; 2017 T833)

Date: c.1600-c.1677.

Description: Silver ring, circular in plan, and D-shaped in section. Its flat exterior is inscribed in italic script: *Sr George Sondes Lees [...]*. The engraving is crude, and the small superscript *r* in the abbreviation of Sir appears to be a correction from a capital letter. 10.21mm x 2.49mm. 0.55g.

Discussion: The individual named upon this vervel is almost certainly Sir George Sondes (1599-1677), 1st Earl Feversham and Viscount Sondes, who lived on the Lees Court Estate (HE: 1000388), where this vervel was found. Although Sondes was MP for Higham Ferrers, Northamptonshire in the 1620s and for Ashburton, Devon after the Restoration, 'he appears to have regarded himself as a Kentishman rather than Member for a Devon constituency, concerning himself with Dover harbour and the Medway navigation, but not with west country bills' (HoP). Sir George was also at the centre of a public tragedy when, in 1655, his eldest son (and heir) was murdered by his brother; when the murderer was convicted and executed, Sir George was left without an heir.

Location: Returned to finder/landowner.

J Ahmet & I Richardson

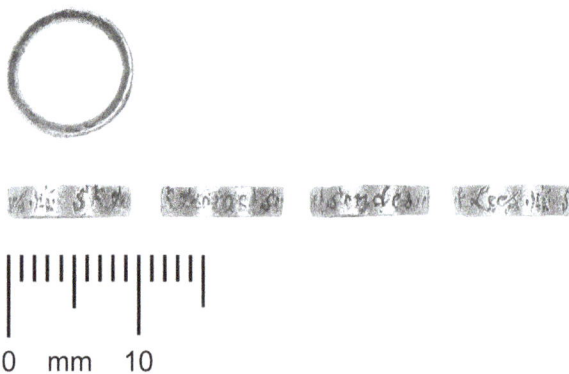

Vervel from Badlesmere (KENT-8DE94E) (courtesy of the Portable Antiquities Scheme).

Lees Court, drawing in the British Museum (© The Trustees of the British Museum).

B11 KENT, CHIDDINGSTONE (KENT-C245C7; 2007 T378)

Date: c.1550-c.1650.

Description: Silver ring, circular in plan, and D-shaped in section. The flat outer face is engraved in serifed captials: OF.NORWOOD.IN.KENT. 11.27mm x 3.8mm. 1.1g.

Discussion: The name 'Norwood' appears in numerous locations in Kent and nearby. It is the name of a residential area of Greater London lying mostly within the modern boroughs of Croydon (which was historically part of the county of Surrey) and Lambeth. These Norwoods derive their name from the great North Wood (BHO), which extended across Croydon and into the London boroughs of Bromley, Lambeth and Lewisham. Norwood is also the shortened name of the manor Northwood Chasteners in the parish of Milton Regis, Kent (probably HE: 1343863) and a manor near Canterbury (BHO). The findspot is not close to any of these. Instead, the nearest architectural landmark is Penshurst Place (HE: 1243139), a 'rambling' 14th-century estate expanded over the years, 1.7km away. In the 16th century this was home to the prominent courtier Sir Philip Sidney (1554-86). On his death the estate transferred to his brother Robert Sidney (1563-1626), 1st Earl of Leicester and Viscount Lisle and has been in the De L'Isle family ever since. It is therefore not known to who's bird this vervel was once fixed.

Location: Returned to finder/landowner.

I Richardson & D Thornton

Vervel from Chiddingstone (KENT-C245C7) (courtesy of the Portable Antiquities Scheme).

B12 KENT, LYDD (KENT-E15F34; 2005 T302)

Date: c.1606-c.1642.

Description: Silver ring, circular in plan, and D-shaped in section. The flat exterior face is inscribed in italic script: *Richa. Hardres Esqr.*. 10mm x 2.85mm x 1.4mm. 0.71g.

Discussion: The most likely owner of this vervel is Sir Richard Hardres (1606–69) of Hardres Court, Upper Hardres, near Canterbury, Kent (HE: 1085512). Sir Richard married Anne Godfrey, and was created a baronet in 1642, which suggests that the vervel dates from before that year (Burke & Burke 1844: 242-3). The Hardres were an eminent family; Hardres Court itself was endowed with a wooden gate from the French city of Bolougne, bestowed upon an ancestor of Sir Richard's by Henry VIII for his assistance in taking that city in 1544. Nonetheless by the 17th century the family had fallen on hard times, and Sir Richard's father, Sir Thomas Hardres (1575-1628), was forced to sell some land in order to pay his creditors (Jenkins 1861: 43-57).

Sir Richard's wife, Anne, was the daughter of either Thomas Godfrey (1553-1625) or his son Peter Godfrey (1580-1624) of Lydd, Kent, the parish where the vervel was found, which lies roughly 37km to the south west of Upper Hardres. The findspot is not close to any substantial historic buildings, but the family connection to Lydd may explain why it was found at such a distance from the Hardres home.

Location: Returned to finder/landowner.

D Pennock, B McLeod & I Richardson

Vervel from Lydd (KENT-E15F34) (courtesy of the Portable Antiquities Scheme).

B13 LEICESTERSHIRE, HALLATON (NARC-C41B23; 2015 T215)

Date: c.1600-c.1700.

Description: Silver ring, circular in plan, and D-shaped in section. The outer face of the ring is flat and inscribed in italic script: *Roulston in leicestershire*. There is a vertical mark on the band, just after the 'n' in the inscription, which appears to be where the two ends of

the ring were joined together. 10mm x 3.5mm x 1.5mm. 0.6g.

Discussion: Roulston is possibly the surname of the owner of the vervel, though convention suggests that as it appears here it is more likely to be a place name. Roulston is a variation on the spelling of Rolleston, a village and civil parish approximately 10km north west of where this vervel was found (not to be confused with Rolleston in Nottinghamshire). The manor of Rolleston was given to Richard and Joan Dixon (dates unknown) of Ilston in 1546 and it continued in the Dixon family until the death of William Dixon in 1628. Thereafter the manor was sold to William Sharpe (d.1658) and then to Henry Greene (d.1680), in whose family it remained until the 19th century (BHO).

Closer to the findspot, approximately 2.6km away, is Keythorpe Hall (HE: 1360674) which was moved to its current location in the 19th-century from a spot that was slightly closer to where the vervel was found. It is possible that the owner of this vervel was visiting a local acquaintance or, given the proximity of his home, that he had simply ventured out from there.

Location: Leicestershire Museums.

I Richardson & J Cassidy

Vervel from Hallaton (NARC-C41B23) (courtesy of the Portable Antiquities Scheme).

B14 NORFOLK, BROOME (NMS-584F18; 2017 T159)

Date: c.1620-c.1708.

Description: Silver ring, circular in plan, and of unknown shape in section. The exterior face is inscribed on the outer face in italic script: {foliate spray} *Broom hall in Norff S.* 9mm. 0.5g.

Discussion: The vervel was discovered in the vicinity of the former Broome Hall (Norfolk HER: 10639), which was built in c.1600, rebuilt later in the 17th century, and demolished in 1825. While some fragments of the building were documented in the late 20th century, cropmarks are the only remaining indication of the site of the estate now (Norfolk HER).

During the 17th century Broom Hall was the residence of Sir William Cook (1600-81), made 1st Baronet of Broome Hall in 1663. His son, another Sir William (1630-1708), who also resided at Broome Hall, was a prominent public figure. He served as Justice of the Peace for Norfolk (1660-8) and was Captain of the Norfolk Militia (1660-79). He served as MP for Great Yarmouth (1685-89) and of Norfolk (1689-1700). This Sir William became the 2nd Baronet upon his father's death in 1681, but from at least 1700 suffered from ill health (gout and kidney or gall stones). From then on, he was unable to attend Parliament, and sold the estate in 1702 to retire to Suffolk to live with his daughter and son-in-law (HoP). Perhaps then, this vervel belonged to a hawking bird owned by one of these two men.

Location: Norwich Castle Museum.

J Shoemark & I Richardson

Vervel from Broome (NMS-584F18) (courtesy of the Portable Antiquities Scheme).

B15 NORFOLK, EPPINGHAM (NMS-236202; 2016 T73)

Date: c.1600-c.1700.

Description: Silver ring, circular in plan, and D-shaped in section. The exterior face is inscribed in serifed capitals: BILNGFORD IN NOR. The F resembles an E. There is a faint transverse line between the G and F, indicating the join in the ring, and the remains of a very worn and now indecipherable mark between the R and B, perhaps a maker's mark, though this would be unusual. 11mm x 2.5mm. 0.57g.

Discussion: The inscription probably refers to Billingford, in the Breckland district of Norfolk, which is approximately 20km south west of the findspot. The nearest major post-medieval property to the find is Blickling Hall (HE: 1051428), which is roughly 3km from where the vervel was found. Blickling Hall was constructed upon the site of an earlier house, between c.1619 and 1627 for Sir Henry Hobart, 1st baronet (c.1554-1625), MP for St Ives (1588-9), Great Yarmouth (1597 and 1601) and Norwich (1604-11), Lord Chief Justice of the Court of Common Pleas (1613-25) and Chancellor to Henry, Prince of Wales (1617-25) etc (DNB; HoP).

Location: Norwich Castle Museum.

E Darch & I Richardson

Vervel from Eppingham (NMS-236202) (courtesy of the Portable Antiquities Scheme).

B16 NORFOLK, WIVETON (NMS-2AE576; 2015 T629)

Date: c.1575-c.1650.

Description: Silver ring, circular in plan, and D-shaped in section. The exterior face is inscribed in serifed captials: {cross} HADLYGE • IN • SVF; a pair of faintly engraved guide lines are visible between the inscribed letters, and also a faint X behind the initial cross. 9mm x 2.5mm. 0.6g.

Discussion: The inscription seems to refer to the town of Hadleigh, in southern Suffolk, 100km south of the place where the vervel was found. This is one of three vervels found within a 2km radius, the others (**Ci05** and **Ci08**) being roughly contemporary (dated between c.1600 and c.1625), and discussed in the introduction.

This area of North Norfolk is not far from several grand homes extant in the 17th century. 1km to the north of the findspot, the current incarnation of Wiveton Hall (HE: 1373519), dates to 1653 by an inscription on one of its doorways, and may have been built after some of the estate was bought by a Mr Gifford of Gloucester. It replaced an earlier building, from the late 13th century, built by the De Roos family (Wiveton Hall History). Also Bayfield Hall (HE: 1152147), the current structure, of 18th century date, having largely replaced a Tudor manor.

Location: Norwich Castle Museum; donated by finder/landowner.

E Darch & I Richardson

Vervel from Wiveton (NMS-2AE576) (courtesy of the Portable Antiquities Scheme).

B17 OXFORDSHIRE, BUCKNELL (BERK-6BD475; 2011 T461)

Date: c.1600-c.1700.

Description: Silver ring, circular in plan, and D-shaped in section. Its flat exterior face is inscribed in serifed capital letters: {possible five-pointed star} OF EDMVNTON. 9.78mm x 2.49mm x 1.25 mm. 0.7g.

Discussion: The inscription is likely to refer to Edmonton, now in North London, 80km south east of the findspot. The mansion house and estate in Pymmes Park, Edmonton, was purchased in 1582 by William Cecil, 1st Baron Burghley (1520-98) and inherited by his son Robert, 1st Earl of Salisbury (1563-1612), and then it remained in the family until sometime before 1804 (BHO). The Cecil Papers of Hatfield House, containing correspondence of Robert Cecil, make specific mention of vervels, but they also reveal that by as early as 1604 the house was being leased out – in this case by a Richard Orrell (CCP: August 1604) and there is no evidence that any of the Cecils would have necessarily used 'Edmunton' to identify something as belonging to them.

Less than 1km away from the findspot is Bucknell Manor (HE: 1046889), parts of which are 17th century, or possibly earlier in date. Ownership of the manor in the 17th century is complex. Upon his death in 1594, Thomas Moyle passed Bucknell manor to his grandson, also Thomas, who, upon his death in 1622, passed it to his second son, another Thomas. He soon sold it to Edward Ewer, who in 1638 left it to his son, including debts taken over from the Moyles. Eventually the manor was taken over by Samuel Trotman in 1652 when Francis Ewer could not pay off these debts. It seems the Trotmans were still in possession of the manor in the early 18th century (BHO).

It is therefore not certain who from Edmonton once owned the hunting bird that lost this vervel, or why it was lost in Bucknell, and upon whose land.

Location: Returned to finder; not Treasure as found prior the Treasure Act 1996.

A Byard, I Richardson & M Lewis

Vervel from Bucknell (BERK-6BD475) (courtesy of the Portable Antiquities Scheme).

B18 SOMERSET, TAUNTON area (SOM-D02D71; 2013 T477)

Date: c.1575-c.1632.

Description: Silver ring, circular in plan, and rectangular in section. Its flat external face is inscribed in serifed capital letters, in two lines: {six-pointed star} RETORNE TOO // {six-pointed star} HVGH {six-pointed star} PORTMAN. 9.3mm x 4.2mm. 0.82g.

Discussion: The findspot is approximately 2km west of Orchard Portman, which gained the second part of its name from the prominent Portman family. Two Hugh Portmans are known to have resided there, at Orchard Portman House; this is now demolished, but once stood northwest of the local church, St Michael's (HE: 1060391). One is Sir Hugh Portman (c.1562-1604), who was MP for Somerset in 1597, and owned ten manors and over 100 houses in Somerset (HoP). Another is Sir Hugh (1607-29), the 4th Baronet Portman, who served as MP for Taunton in 1625 and 1628-9. He was only 17 when he first returned for Taunton, but he died young and was buried in the chancel at St Michael's, Orchard Portman (HoP).

Interestingly, a gold seal matrix (SOM-19831E) featuring the arms of Sir John Portman (1570-1612) combined with those of his wife Anne Gifford (d.1638), the parents of Hugh, the 4th baronet, was discovered in the same general area by the same metal-detectorist.

Location: Museum of Somerset.

R Webley, I Richardson & M Lewis

Vervel from Taunton area (SOM-D02D71) (courtesy of the Portable Antiquities Scheme).

Gold seal matrix of Sir John Portman (SOM-19831E) (courtesy of the Portable Antiquities Scheme).

B19 SUFFOLK, FRESSINGFIELD (SF-1A876D; 2016 T901)

Date: c.1650-c.1701.

Description: Silver ring, circular in plan, and D-shaped in section. The flat external face is inscribed in italics: *John Hanmer Esq of Wittinghã: hall*. The internal face is curved. 12.96mm x 3.05mm x 1.27mm. 1.06g.

Discussion: This vervel almost certainly belonged to a hunting bird of Sir John Hanmer (d. 1701), 3rd Baronet of Hanmer, Flintshire, and Whittingham Hall, Fressingfield, Suffolk (HE: 1032964). He was MP for Flint (1659, and 1685-90), Evesham (1669-79) and Flintshire (1681-5), and also served with King William III at the Battle of the Boyne (1690).

Whittingham Hall had come into the Hanmer family through Sir John's mother, Elizabeth Baker. It was then formally inherited by Sir John, upon the death of his father (Sir Thomas), in 1678 and then passed down through his family until c.1764, when it came into the possession of Sir William Bunbury (Suffolk HER: FSF 007). The vervel was found in close proximity to the Hall.

John Hanmer was knighted at the time of the Restoration (1660), so presumably, given the absence of this title in the inscription, the vervel pre-dates that event, though that is by no means certain. Hanmer also served as 'Esquire of the Body' (a role which was once a personal attendant of the monarch but by the 17th century had become an honorary position) between 1670 and 1685, so possibly the vervel is referencing that position (HoP); again this is just supposition, as other vervels have 'Esq' upon them. He died in a duel in 1701, leaving no issue.

Location: Returned to finder/landowner.

A Booth & I Richardson

Vervel from Fressingfield (SF-1A876D) (courtesy of the Portable Antiquities Scheme).

B20 SUFFOLK, THORNDON (SF-C546B8; 2017 T424)

Date: c.1575-c.1650.

Description: Silver ring, circular in plan, and rectangular in section. Its external face is flat and inscribed in serifed capitals: {six-pointed star} SHELFORDE {five-pointed star} OF[?]. The first H and E are ligated. The internal face flat and plain. 10.72 x 3.44mm x 1.61mm. 1.08g.

Discussion: The name Shelford appears to have few obvious associations with the parish of Thorndon, where this vervel was found. The origins of the name probably lie in Cambridgeshire where the villages of Great and Little Shelford are located. A Shelford House (HE: 1182523) is also located near Lavenham, Suffolk, but this is some 25km distant south west of the findspot.

The vervel was found nearby the moated manor of Hestley Hall, Thorndon (HE: 1215487), and this connection might better explain the vervel's loss there. Parts of this manor farmhouse date to the first half of the 16th century. Between the second half of the 16th century and early 17th century, Hestley was owned by the Prettyman family, but their connection with Shelford is unknown.

Location: Returned to finder/landowner.

A Booth & I Richardson

Vervel from Thorndon (SF-C546B8) (courtesy of the Portable Antiquities Scheme).

B21 SUSSEX (EAST), BATTLE (SUSS-B72845; 2006 T60)

Date: c.1600-c.1700.

Description: Silver ring, sub-circular in plan, and rectangular in section; flattened, with engraved lines at both edges. The face is abraded, and the inscription cannot be read with any certainty, though it appears to read, DE L'ARGENT, incised in serifed block capitals, preceded by an ovoid figure containing a saltire within. The form of this ring departs from the more commonly seen examples (e.g. **B03** and **B04**) that are thicker and D-shaped in section. 5.9mm x 0.98. 1.34g.

Discussion: The meaning of *De L'Argent* is unclear, but it may be a reference to the French word for 'money'; it does not appear to have a familial connection with the local area. Listed buildings are to be found in the vicinity of the findspot, but none have any clear associations with this vervel.

Location: Battle Museum.

L Andrews-Wilson, D Thornton & I Richardson

Vervel from Battle (SUSS-B72845) (courtesy of the Portable Antiquities Scheme).

B22 YORKSHIRE (NORTH), DUNNINGTON (YORYM-2FB222; 2007 T183)

Date: c.1550-c.1610.

Description: Silver ring, circular in plan, and rectangular in section. The exterior face is roughly inscribed with Roman serifed capitals: {?six-pointed star} IAMES BERKBE: . c.9mm.

Discussion: It is possible that the inscription refers to James Birkby (1557-1610), who served as MP for York in 1593 and 1597, and held other public offices, including sheriff and lord mayor. He was the son of another James Birkby (dates unknown) and possibly an Alyce Byrkebye (d.1562). By the turn of the century it is reported 'that he being too old and unwieldy could not ride with less than two men', which implies that any outdoor pursuits would have been tiring affairs (HoP).

It seems that James Birkby owned extensive lands around York, and in West Yorkshire (ibid), which might explain

this vervel's loss in Dunnington, to the east of York, but it is not certain why. To the northeast and southwest of the findspot are Dunnington and Grimston, both with manors which have now gone, presumably superseded by modern buildings, perhaps including Dunnington Hall (HE: 1301178), Grimston Hill (HE: 1148514) and Manor Farmhouse (HE: 1166843). In 1548 the manor at Dunnington was 'let by the prebendary' to John Boyce (seemingly) until 1692, and that at Grimston to William Tanckard in 1599, who still held the manor house by 1630 (BHO).

Location: Returned to finder/landowner.

L Andrews-Wilson, D Thornton, M Lewis & I Richardson

Vervel from Dunnington (YORYM-2FB222) (courtesy of the Portable Antiquities Scheme).

Type C (Ring with Shield) Vervels

Type Ci: Ring with Shield-Shaped Plates Attached Vertically

England

Ci01 BEDFORDSHIRE, BLETSOE (NARC811)

Date: c.1526-c.1558, or possibly later.

Description: Silver ring, circular in plan, and D-shaped in section. Its exterior face is inscribed in serifed capital letters: SEYNT {?five-pointed star} IOHN. Attached vertically to the ring, opposite the inscription, is a shield-shaped plate, where the ring is joined. This is engraved with a coat-of-arms: *a bend and in chief two stars*. Ring: 11.88mm; Shield: 8.94mm x 7.35mm x 3.27mm. 1.36g.

Discussion: The arms upon the vervel are those of one of a number of St Johns of Bletsoe (Clive Cheesman, *pers. comm.*): *argent, a bend gules on a chief of the last two mullets or*. The first to claim them was Oliver St John (d.1437) (Chesshyre & Woodcock 1992: 367-8), more of which below. His great-grandson Sir John St John of Bletsoe (fl.1495-1558) was MP for Bedfordshire in 1529-36 (probably), 1539-40 and 1542-4, and was knighted in 1526. In 1537 he was accused of hunting without permission on land owned by Lord Mountjoy, near one of his own properties in Northamptonshire (HoP). His son, Sir Oliver St John (1522-82), was MP for Bedfordshire (1547-52), High Sheriff of Bedfordshire and Buckinghamshire (1551) and Lord Lieutenant of Bedfordshire (1560-69), in addition to numerous other roles performed in royal service. Oliver had ten children, including John (d.1596), who was the 2nd Baron St John of Bletso and also MP for Bedfordshire (1559 & 1563-7), and Oliver (c.1540-1618), who was the 3rd Baron.

The vervel was found close to the remains of Bletsoe Castle (HE: 1012365), a moated medieval site of which the extant manor dates to the late 16th century (HE: 1114219). In 1086 (Domesday) the manor belonged to Hugh de Beauchamp, passing to the St Johns, when the heiress to the manor, Margaret (c.1410-82), married the above-mentioned Sir Oliver St John (d.1437). The findspot and content of the inscription therefore present a wide range of individuals with whom this vervel might be associated.

Location: Returned to finder; not Treasure as found prior to the Treasure Act 1996.

R Harte, I Richardson & M Lewis

Vervel from Bletsoe (NARC811) (courtesy of the Portable Antiquities Scheme).

Ci02 BUCKINGHAMSHIRE, PRINCES RISBOROUGH (BH-D528FA; 2015 T216)

Date: c.1628-c.1643.

Description: Silver ring, circular in plan, and D-shaped in section. Its exterior face is inscribed in italic script: *Robert Erle Carmarvin*. Attached vertically to the ring, opposite the inscription, is a shield-shaped plate. This is engraved with the image of a bird with outstretched arms perched upon a crude depiction of a gloved hand, with a crown above. Ring: 7.85mm. Shield: 8.23mm. 1.04g.

Discussion: The device on the shield of this vervel is the crest of Robert Dormer (1610-1643), 1st Earl of Carnarvon, and represents *A falconer's right-hand glove fesswise, argent, thereon a falcon, wings inverted also argent, belled and beaked or* (Burke 1884: 293). Robert received the title Baron Dormer aged about six, and then, in 1628, was raised to Viscount Ascott and Earl of Carnarvon. During the English Civil War he died at the first Battle of Newbury (20 September 1643) fighting for the King. Both Robert's crest, and the vervel itself, reinforce his fondness, before the War, for hunting, hawking and field sports (DNB).

Robert Dormer had several connections with the area in which the vervel was found. In 1641 he was appointed Lord Lieutenant of Buckinghamshire and served in that role until his death thereafter being buried in the family vault at All Saint's church, Wing, Buckinghamshire (DNB). Some 12km north of the findspot is Eythrope (HE: 1001397), a former Dormer family estate, but only 1km away is Horsenden Manor (HE:1125830). The current house dates from the 19th century, but in the 17th century the manor was owned by royalist Sir John Denham (BHO), and perhaps this connection explains the vervel's loss nearby.

Location: Buckinghamshire County Museum.

R Paul & I Richardson

Robert Dormer, engraving in the British Museum (©The Trustees of the British Museum).

Ci03 CAMBRIDGESHIRE, CHILDERLEY
(LEIC-224E74; 2014 T307)

Date: c.1575-c.1646.

Description: Silver ring, circular in plan, and D-shaped in section. Its exterior face is inscribed in italic script: *John Cuts*. Attached vertically to the ring, opposite the inscription, is a shield-shaped plate. This is engraved with a crest showing a collared greyhound, erased, above a torse (a heraldic wreath). Ring: 9mm x 3mm; Shield: 12mm x 9mm. 1.24g.

Discussion: The crest upon the vervel is that of several members of the Cutts family of Childerley Hall (HE: 1000614): *a greyhound's head erased argent, collared gules, ringed or* (Burke 1884: 255). The epigraphy of the inscription closely parallels that on **Ci05**, which can be more precisely dated, therefore suggesting that the vervel belongs to a bird of one of two Sir John Cutts, although there are later family members with the same name.

The first (1545-1615), was Sheriff of Cambridgeshire and Huntingdonshire (1572-73) and a Member of Parliament for Cambridgeshire in 1584, 1586 and 1601 (HoP). His grandmother, Luce Browne, was a daughter of Sir Anthony Browne (1443-1506), meaning he was distant cousin to

the likely owner of **B06** above. In the late 16th century this Sir John constructed the aforementioned Childerley Hall, for which he cleared and depopulated the villages of Great Childerley and Little Childerley (including their medieval churches). This building is less than 1km away from the findspot. He was also the keeper of Somersham Palace (HE:1014075), 10km north of the findspot, which transferred from the Bishops of Ely to the Crown in 1600. King James I found Somersham to be a suitable place for hunting and after a visit in 1604 he wrote to Sir John to make the park ready for hunting in the following year (BHO).

The second possible owner of the vervel was Sir John's son, John (1581-1646), who was also a MP for Cambridgeshire on several occasions between 1604 and 1640; although no Parliaments convened between 1629 and 1640. He was knighted in 1603. Following the death of this John, his widow Anne controlled the estate until their son, another John, came of age, in 1655. During this period, on 6-7 June 1647, King Charles I was brought to Childerley Hall after being captured by Parliamentary forces in nearby Northamptonshire.

Location: Returned to landowner; kept at Childerley Hall.

S Hall, I Richardson & W Scott

Vervel from Childerley (LEIC-224E74) (courtesy of the Portable Antiquities Scheme).

Ci04 LINCOLNSHIRE, GAYTON-LE-WOLD (NLM-03EDD2; 2004 T123)

Date: c.1600-c.1634.

Description: Silver ring, circular in plan, and D-shaped in section. Its flat exterior face is inscribed in serifed capitals: SR. WIL. HANSARD. Attached vertically to the ring, opposite the inscription, is a shield-shaped plate. This is engraved with the image of an arm extending upwards from a bar, gripping a six-pointed star between the thumb and two forefingers. Ring: 10.75mm. 1.28g.

Discussion: The most likely candidate for the owner of the hawk to which this vervel was attached is Sir William Hansard (d.1634) of Gayton, who was the great grandson of Thomas Hansard of Wickenby; their crest was *a cubit arm erect vested or, holding in the hand proper, a mullet argent* (Gibbons 1898: 43-4). The aforementioned Sir

William is named as the son and executor of the will of Christobell Lacon of Biscathrope, proved 1611 (Maddison 1891: 58-9). He was also the defendant in a case involving the manor of Biscathorpe and property in Gayton, Lincolnshire between 1621 and 1625 (NA: Compton v Hazard, C 3/339/3). Presumably it was this same William Hansard of Biscathorpe (part of the parish of Gayton le Wold) who was a benefactor of Caistor Grammar School in Lincolnshire in 1634.

The only traces of a 17th century residence in the vicinity of the findspot of the vervel is Grimblethorpe Hall (HE: 1063140) approximately 1km away, but there is no obvious connection between that property and the Hansards. Gayton Manor House (HE: 1063139), a 19th century building less than 1km from the findspot, probably replaced an earlier building and may have been part of the estate of the Hansards of Biscathope and Gayton.

Location: Returned to finder/landowner; subsequently sold privately.

D Thornton & I Richardson

Vervel from Gayton-le-Wold (NLM-03EDD2) (courtesy of the Portable Antiquities Scheme).

Ci05: NORFOLK, CLEY NEXT THE SEA
(NMS-82AD63; 2012 T88)

Date: c.1600-c.1612.

Description: Silver ring, circular in plan, D-shaped in section. The flat exterior face is inscribed in italic script: *Henrye Prince {7-pointed star}*. Attached vertically to the ring, opposite the inscription, is a shield-shaped plate; the ends of the (ring) band are butted together. The shield is engraved with the badge of the Prince of Wales: three ostrich feathers enfiled by a coronet and passing through a scroll bearing the words ICH DIEN. Ring: 10.5mm x 3mm; Shield: 9mm x 8mm x 0.5mm. 1.37g.

Discussion: The badge and inscription upon the vervel refers to Henry Frederick (1594-1612), son of King James I of England (1566-1625) and Anne of Denmark (1574-1619). Henry was created Prince of Wales in 1610, though he was known to use this royal insignia of the heir designate several years prior to his investment (MacLeod & Wilks 2013: 94-5). His father's fondness for the pursuit of game was well known, and Henry himself is depicted at a young age in a dramatic portrait of 1603 by Robert Peake the Elder, standing over a fallen deer and sheathing his sword, a hunting dog lying patiently behind him, while his companion Sir John Harington holds the deer's antlers (ibid); this however may have only been part of the creation of an idealised image of the prince. After his death, one of his many eulogizers told of an incident where the Prince attended his father's lodge at Royston, Hertfordshire, and complained to the King about his obsession with the hunt; one which Henry did not share (Strong 2000: 25-7). Prince Henry died of typhoid fever in 1612, and therefore it was his younger brother, Charles (1600-1649), who became king as Charles I.

It is not known why this vervel is likely to have been lost at Cley next the Sea. There is no evidence that the young prince ever visited – though the findspot is very close to **B15** and **Ci08**, the entries for which discuss the great houses in the area.

Location: Norwich Castle Museum.

E Darch, S Ashley & I Richardson

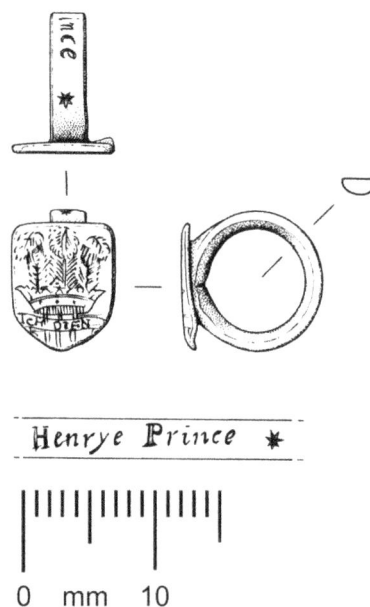

Vervel from Cley next the Sea (NMS-82AD63) (courtesy of the Portable Antiquities Scheme).

Ci06 NORFOLK, PULHAM MARKET
(NMS-F39863; 2011 T858)

Date: c.1600-c.1700.

Description: Silver ring, circular in plan, and D-shaped in section. The exterior face of the band is inscribed in semi-italic script *Edward Hunne*. Attached vertically to the ring, opposite the inscription, is a shield-shaped plate: the sides of the shield have since been crimped around the edge of the ring. The shield is engraved with a lion rampant, now worn. Ring: 9.5mm x 3mm; Shield 4mm. 0.54g.

Discussion: The family of Hunne, of Ilketshall St Margaret, Suffolk, bore arms of *azure, a lion rampant guardant, argent* (Corder 1965: column 44), so this vervel might be connected with an Edward Hunne of that family, although no memorials of him appear in the local parish church (BHO). Ilketshall St Margaret is roughly 15km east from the vervel findspot, so it is not readily apparent why it was lost at Pulham Market. Furthermore, there are no surviving great houses of the 16th or 17th century in the immediate vicinity. It is known, however, that the parish of Forncett, situated 9km to the north west of the findspot, had as its rectors of (either or both) St Peters and St Marys, from 1615 to 1617, a certain Thomas and Edward Hunne (BHO), the latter of whom might be associated with this vervel.

Location: Norwich Castle Museum.

E Darch, S Ashley, & I Richardson

Vervel from Pulham Market (NMS-F39863) (courtesy of the Portable Antiquities Scheme).

Ci07 NORFOLK, SPIXWORTH (NMS-973788; 2009 T44)

Date: 1643.

Description: Flat, silver, shield-shaped plate, inscribed WC 1643 on one side, within an engraved linear border with multiple transverse lines. On the reverse, the heads of two separate silver rivets, flush with the front face, are bent over. Shield: 12.5mm x 12mm x 0.5mm. 0.62g.

Discussion: This is probably part of a vervel, although normally the shield-shaped plate is joined to a rectangular or D-shaped section ring with solder. In this case, the remains of the ring (if that is what it is) appears more like a wire loop, such as on a button rather than a vervel.

The letters and numbers engraved on the front of the shield are probably an owner's initials and the date of manufacture, though they are unusual for this type of vervel, with most having a crest or badge. That said, the size and weight of the shield support the idea that it is component of a vervel, even if its ring is composed differently.

The item was found less than 1km from the former Spixworth Hall, a 17th century mansion built by William Peck in 1607 and demolished in 1950. A barn (HE:1050874) on the site is all that remains of the building fabric from that period. If this object is connected with that Hall then it is not clear how the initials upon it relate.

Location: Norwich Castle Museum.

A Rogerson & I Richardson

Vervel from Spixworth (NMS-973788) (courtesy of the Portable Antiquities Scheme).

Ci08 NORFOLK, WIVETON (PAS-DABAFB; 2006 T231)

Date: c.1575-c.1625.

Description: Silver ring, circular in plan, and D-shaped in section. The flat exterior face is inscribed in semi-italic script: *Tho. Gryme. of.* Attached vertically to the ring, opposite the inscription, is a shield-shaped plate; a small gap exists between the ends of the ring at the junction with the plate. The shield is engraved three times with the letter T, two side-by-side above a slightly larger example. Ring: 8.5mm; Shield: 8.5mm x 7mm. 1.02g.

Discussion: The motif upon the vervel is the arms of the Grime family of Trimingham, Antingham and Suffield, Norfolk: *azure three cross taus or* (Rye 1913: 271), although no tincture survives. The owner of the object was almost certainly Thomas Gryme, lord of the manor of Antingham, whose will was proved in 1591. His second son was also called Thomas (Hoare 1918: 391). It is unlikely that he would have born the arms undifferenced, so this vervel could be associated with either individual.

Antingham is roughly 25 km south east from the findspot. Found in the same vicinity, however, are **B15** (800m away) and **Ci05** (1400m). Several historic properties are found in the area, as mentioned above; the mid-17th century Wiveton Hall (HE: 1373519) is approximately 1km away, while Bayfield Hall (HE: 1152147), dating from the 16th century, lies almost 2km distant. Bayfield Hall was owned from the early 1400s by the Yelverton/Clares. In 1634, Sir Henry Yelverton was Lord of the Manor; he appears to be a different Sir Henry to the Attorney-General and MP for Northampton (1566-1629). After Yelverton the property passed to Robert Jermy Esq (dates unknown), who was lord in 1661, and it continued down his line (Blomefield 1808). It is therefore unclear how the vervel is directly connected to either of these two places.

Location: Norwich Castle Museum.

A Rogerson & I Richardson

Vervel from Wiveton (PAS-DABAFB) (courtesy of the Portable Antiquities Scheme).

Ci09 NORTHAMPTONSHIRE, LOWICK (LEIC-EC7A73; 2010 T413)

Date: c.1470-c.1700.

Description: Silver ring, circular in plan (but now distorted), rectangular in section, and plain on both sides. Attached vertically to the ring is a shield-shaped plate, where the two ends join. The shield is engraved with a Stafford knot, above which sits the initials 'I S' in serifed capital script. Shield: 11mm x 8mm x 5mm. 0.67g.

Discussion: The Stafford knot is associated not only with the parish and county of the same name, but also the Stafford family. Several Staffords owned Drayton Manor (HE: 1001031) in Lowick, approximately 2km from where this vervel was found. John Stafford, 1st Earl of Wiltshire (1427-1473) inherited Drayton Hall from his father-in-law in 1467, and upon his death it passed to his son, Edward (1470-99) (BHO). It is therefore possible, though not certain, that that the initials 'I S' upon this vervel stand for John Stafford, which would make this one of the earliest in this catalogue. John Stafford was the youngest son of Humphrey, the 1st Duke of Buckingham (1402-60), who was a military commander in both the Hundred Years' War and the Wars of the Roses. While Humphrey was killed fighting for the Lancastrians at the Battle of Northampton (1460), John fought on the Yorkist side at Hexham (1464). He was made Earl of Wiltshire in 1470, and made a Knight of the Garter two years later. The estate passed to his son Edward (1470-1499), who has a memorial in St Peter's Church, Lowick, itself only a few hundred metres from the findspot. After Edward's death the property passed to John Mordaunt, 1st Baron Mordaunt (d.1562).

The style of writing on the vervel, however, could be later than late-15th Century and therefore the association with John Stafford is only supposed.

Location: Returned to finder/landowner.

I Richardson, W Scott & S Hall

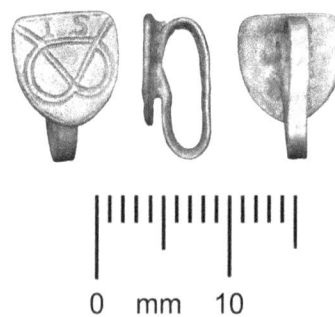

Vervel from Lowick (LEIC-EC7A73) (courtesy of the Portable Antiquities Scheme).

Tomb of Edward Stafford in St Peter's, Lowick
(© Andrew Abbott).

Vervel from Angmering (SUSS-D17951) (courtesy of the
Portable Antiquities Scheme).

Ci10 SUSSEX (WEST), ANGMERING
(SUSS-D17951; 2017 T10)

Date: c.1603-c.1625.

Description: Silver ring, circular in plan, and D-shaped
in section. The flat exterior face of the ring is inscribed
in italic script: *Kyng James.* Attached vertically to the
ring, opposite the inscription, is a shield shaped plate;
this is damaged at the edges, having been bent over and
in one place broken away. The shield is engraved with the
Stuart Royal Arms (outside of Scotland), used between the
accession of James I as king of England in 1603 and the
death of Anne in 1707. 9mm x 5mm. 0.9g.

Discussion: The vervel is similar in appearance and size
to **Cii04**, found at Thwaite Hall, Suffolk, and now in the
collection of the British Museum (2000,0701.1), although
the shield attaches to the ring horizontally. It features the
same coat of arms, but is inscribed *King Charlles*.

Angmering, where this vervel was found, has no obvious
connection with either James I (r.1603-25) or his grandson
James II (r.1685-88). The findspot is close to Ham Manor
(HE: 1027689), owned mostly by the Gratwicke family
in the early 17th century, and about 1km from the former
New Place (HE: 1232882), a late 16th century manor
house built by Sir Thomas Palmer and sold to Sir Thomas
Bishopp, 1st Baronet, in 1615. The latter's main residence
was at Parham Park (HE: 1027355), which is about 10km
north of the place where the vervel was found. According
to John Nichols (1828: 613), 'there is a tradition in the
family at Parham, that Sir Thomas Bishopp was honoured
by a visit from King James, but no certain information on
the subject has been discovered'.

Given the length of his reign, and his known love of hunting,
it seems more probable that the vervel is linked with King
James I, though any association he might have with the
findspot remains a mystery. It is possible that the vervel just
denotes that the bird to which it was attached was a Royal
hawk belonging to the King, rather than one flown by him.

Location: Returned to finder/landowner.

I Richardson & E Wood

King James I and VI, engraving in the British Museum (©
The Trustees of the British Museum).

Ci11 WILTSHIRE, COLLINGBOURNE KINGSTON
(WILT-B08B32; 2012 T670)

Date: c.1540-c.1630.

Description: Silver ring, circular in plan, trapezoidal in
section, with a flat, plain, outer face. Attached vertically
to the ring is a shield-shaped plate, where it joins and is
flattened. The shield is engraved with an image of a two-
legged horned and winged creature, probably a wyvern,
standing left on a torse. Ring: 9.73mm x 2.05mm x
1.35mm. Shield: 9.61mm x 6.80mm x 1.03mm. 1.04g.

Discussion: The depiction on the shield appears to match
that of the heraldic crest of the Herbert family, Earls of
Pembroke, described as *a wyvern with wings elevated vert,
holding in the mouth a sinister hand couped at the wrist*

gules (Fairbairn 1905: 271 & 438).[1] The family seat was at Wilton House, Salisbury (HE: 1023762), about 25km to the south west of the findspot of this vervel.

A very similar vervel, found very nearby, is listed as **Ci12**. During the 16th and 17th centuries, the powerful Seymour family owned three manors and substantial lands inside the modern parish of Collingbourne Kingston, where this vervel was found, though the family seat was at Wulfhall (HE: 1300523) about 10km to the north. The closest extant period building is Sunton House (HE: 1285379), in close proximity to the findspot, though this was built in the early 18th century. However, it may be at the centre of the old Sunton Manor, which was sold by one William Thornhill to Edward Seymour, 1st Duke of Somerset (c.1500-52) in 1548. Although Somerset's property was confiscated when he was executed for treason in 1552, it was returned to his son Sir Edward (1539-1621) in 1553 and remained in the family until the 20th century (BHO).

Sir William Herbert (1507-70) was granted Wilton Abbey in 1540, which he tore down to construct Wilton House. He was a contemporary of the 1st Duke of Somerset, whom he initially supported in his role as Lord Protector of the Realm, upon the death of Henry VIII in 1547, and Somerset's brother, Thomas Seymour (1508-49). Herbert was married to Anne Parr (1515-52), sister of Henry VIII's widow Catherine Parr (1512-48), who in the same year as Henry's death married Thomas Seymour, further connecting the Herberts and Seymours. However, by 1550 Herbert's military success in suppressing the Western Rebellion in 1549 led to increasing influence and probably inevitable tension with Somerset, who allegedly planned to arrest Herbert. Instead it was Somerset who was arrested and thrown in the tower in 1551, after which Herbert was made 1st Earl of Pembroke (of the 10th creation), and Somerset was executed in the following year. In that same year (1552), Pembroke hosted the King at his estate in Wilton (HoP; Sil 2001: 119-27).

Wilton House still remains in the ownership of the Herbert family – the current holder is the 18th Earl of Pembroke. William Herbert, the 3rd Earl (1580-1630), was a favourite of King James I, a patron of William Shakespeare, and Chancellor of Oxford University; he founded Pembroke College, Oxford, with James I. When he died his title passed to his brother Philip, the 4th Earl (1584-1650), another favourite of James I and his son, King Charles I. Philip reportedly hosted Charles at Wilton House for a yearly hunting expedition.

Like much nobility in the Tudor and Stuart periods many of the Herberts seemed to enjoy hunting (and presumably, hawking). It is not possible to know which of the Herberts the vervel might have belonged to but the form suggests it is likely to have been one of the earliest. Given the proximity of the findspot to property owned by the Seymours, it is

tempting to think that it might have been lost in the decade before the 1st Earl of Pembroke and 1st Duke of Somerset had their fatal falling out, however the actual circumstance of its loss (as with **Ci12**) remains unclear.

In an interesting quirk, another of the manors in this parish, Collingbourne Valence, was held between 1253-1324 by two Earls of Pembroke from an earlier creation, William de Valence (late 1220s-96) and his son, Aymer de Valence (c.1275-1324) (BHO).

Location: Returned to finder/landowner.

I Richardson & K Hinds

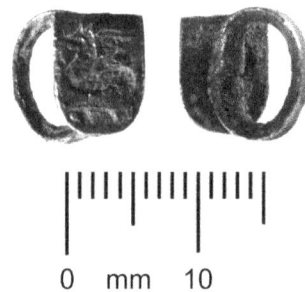

Vervel from Collingbourne Kingston (WILT-B08B32) (courtesy of the Portable Antiquities Scheme).

William Herbert, 3rd Earl of Pembroke, engraving in the British Museum (© The Trustees of the British Museum).

---

[1] The crest of William Herbert, 3rd Earl of Pembroke (1580-1630), can be viewed in the armorial bindings in the collection of the University of Toronto Libraries (British Armorial Bindings 2017).

Ci12 WILTSHIRE, COLLINGBOURNE KINGSTON (WILT-E0B23A; 2016 T284)

Date: c.1580-c.1630.

Description: Silver ring, circular in plan, D-shaped in section, with a flat, plain, outer face. Attached vertically to the ring is a shield-shaped plate where it joins and is flattened. The shield is engraved with an image of a two-legged horned and winged creature, probably a wyvern, standing left on a torse. Ring: 9.24mm. Shield: 8.12mm x 6.51mm x 1.05mm. 1.09g

Discussion: As with **Ci11**, the depiction on the shield appears to match the heraldic crest of the Herberts, Earls of Pembroke, whose founding member, Sir William Herbert (1507-1570) had his seat at Wilton House, 25km to the south west of the findspot.

This vervel was found 600m away from the other (**Ci11**). Given the proximity of the two, and their close resemblance, it seems likely that they were used, and lost, around the same time. It would be unlikely that two separate birds would have flown from Wilton and both lost their vervels in Collingbourne Kingston. Equally, it seems unlikely (given their form) that both vervels come from the same bird. Therefore, it can be assumed that one of the Herberts, or someone in charge of their birds, was flying them in the local area, but the local connection remains unclear.

Location: Wiltshire Museum.

I Richardson & Cristina Sanna

Vervel from Collingbourne Kingston (WILT-E0B23A) (courtesy of the Portable Antiquities Scheme).

Ci13 WORCESTERSHIRE, STOURPORT-ON-SEVERN (WMID-F362CD; 2014 T563)

Date: c.1575-c.1700.

Description: Silver ring, circular in plan, and D-shaped in section. Its flat exterior face is inscribed in serifed capital letters: E. EYTON. OF. Attached vertically to the ring, opposite the inscription, is a shield-shaped plate where its two ends meet. The shield is engraved with a fret: *knot, saltire within lozenge*. Ring: 10.4mm x 3.3mm x 1.5mm. Shield: 10.1mm x 8.1mm x 1.0mm. 1.8g

Discussion: Although without tincture, the arms can be interpreted as *or a fret azure, identified with* the Eyton family of Eyton-on-the-Weald Moors, Shropshire (as

opposed to Eyton on Severn, in the same county, and several other places called Eyton in the Welsh borders). The individual named in the inscription is hard to identify given just a first name initial. There was a seventh son of the Eyton family in the 16th century called either Edmund or Edward, but it is unlikely to have been him because the form and style of the vervel and its inscription suggest that it was more likely made in the 17th century. An alternative association, but also unlikely because of the object's likely date, is with a different family at Gaddesby, Leicestershire, who used the same arms and were headed by an Edward Eyton in the later 16th century. Therefore, the owner of the hawk that lost this vervel is more likely to be an as yet unidentified member of the Shropshire family, though Eyton-on-the Weald Moors and Eyton on Severn are both more than 50km from the findspot.

The closest surviving great house to the findspot is Hartlebury Castle (HE: 1000884), now Worcestershire County Museum, 3.5km to the north east, but there is no apparent connection between the historic building and the Eytons. Closer still, less than 1km away, is Grove Farmhouse (HE: 1215538), which dates to the early-mid 17th century, but again without any known association with the Eyton family.

Another point of consideration is that the Eytons usually quartered their shield with another coat of arms (standing for a family they were descended from in the female line). This does not appear here. This may well be because the vervel is very small and the engraver decided simply to show the unquartered arms.

Location: Museums Worcestershire.

C Cheesman, T Gilmore & I Richardson

Vervel from Stourport-on-Severn (WMID-F362CD) (courtesy of the Portable Antiquities Scheme).

Type Cii: Rings with Shield-Shaped Plates
Attached Horizontally

Cii01 NORFOLK, COLNEY (NMS-D15F32; 2005 T197)

Date: c.1575-c.1650.

Description: Silver ring, circular in plan, and D-shaped in section. Its flat exterior face is inscribed in semi-italic script: {eight-pointed star} *W / Sydnor*. Attached horizontally to the ring is a shield-shaped plate. This is engraved with a *gryphon sejant to dexter* on a crest wreath. The band of the ring is bent up towards the top of the shield. Ring: 6mm. 1.55g.

Discussion: The crest upon the vervel is possibly that of the Sydnors of Blundeston, Suffolk (Cheesman 2012: 48). The manor of Blundeston was conveyed to a William Sydnor (d.1612) in 1570. He had a son, Henry, who died in 1611. When the eldest William died in 1612, his grandson (and eldest male heir), another William Sydnor (d.1632), inherited the manor of Blundeston and associated properties in the surrounding area (BHO).

The findspot of the vervel, just to the west of Norwich, is more than 25km from Blundeston. However, the Sydnors did have connections with Norwich, as the elder William left money for the poor of Conisford at the Gate (Norwich) in his will (BHO), so it is likely that he spent some time in the vicinity. Near to the findspot, is Colney Hall (HE: 1050758), but this dates to the second part of the 18th century. Further away, and to the south, is The Old Hall (HE: 1050756), which is of 17th century date, but with no known association with the Sydnors. It is therefore a mystery how this vervel came to be lost at Colney.

Location: Returned to finder/landowner.

S Ashley & I Richardson

Vervel from Colney (NMS-D15F32) (courtesy of the Portable Antiquities Scheme).

Cii02 NORFOLK, WEREHAM (NMS-A95326; 2008 T692)

Date: c.1550-c.1700.

Description: Silver plate, broadly shield-shaped, but not in the 'heater' style common in most Type C vervels. Rather, its form more closely resembles a Swiss escutcheon, where the top is scalloped and the base pointed. The decoration upon the shield consists of an engraved outline of a cross (quarter-pierced) and a contour line that traces the outline of the shield. On the reverse, towards its base, is a horizontal scar indicating the place of attachment with the ring (now lost). 13.5mm x 11.5mm x 1.5mm. 1.64g

Discussion: The vervel was found in the vicinity of Winnold House (HE: 1077747). This was on the site of a chantry owned by the Priory of West Dereham until it was supressed in 1539 during the Reformation, whence the lands were granted to Mary FitzRoy, Duchess of Richmond (1519-57), widow of Henry VIII's only acknowledged illegitimate son, Henry FitzRoy (1519-36) and daughter of Thomas Howard, 3rd Duke of Norfolk (1473-1554). Upon Mary's death the estate was granted to Thomas Guybon (or Gybbons, d.1605) of King's Lynn, Norfolk, who arranged the construction of the present house (which has since been further modified). However, the simply executed arms on the shield do not appear to be associated with any of these people.

Location: Norwich Castle Museum.

E Darch, A Rogerson & I Richardson

Vervel from Wereham (NMS-A95326) (courtesy of the Portable Antiquities Scheme).

Cii03 SHROPSHIRE, WORFIELD (HESH-3A6AE5; 2009 T508)

Date: c.1550-c.1650.

Description: Silver ring, circular in plan, and D-shaped in section. Its flat exterior face is inscribed in capital letters: IOHN TALBOT; the letters H and N are ligated. Attached horizontally to the band, opposite the inscription, is a shield-shaped plate. The shield is engraved with an image of a hound, or *talbot, passant*. Ring: 8mm. Shield: 8mm x 6mm.

Discussion: The talbot was a type of hunting dog which featured prominently in heraldic achievements. It served as a crest and/or supporter for various members of the Talbot family at different times; for instance the arms of the Earls of Shrewsbury are recorded by Burke (1884: 995) as having *two talbots argent* as supporters.

Sir John Talbot, 10th Earl of Shrewsbury (1601-54) is one possible owner of the hawk that lost this vervel. However, there are many other members of the Talbot family who were given the name John, including Sir John Talbot of Albrighton, Shropshire (c.1485-49), who married twice and had two sons named Sir John; one of Grafton, Worcestershire (c.1513-55), and the other of Salwarp, Worcestershire (1549-81). This latter was grandfather to a George Talbot of Rudge (dates unknown) (Cracrofts Peerage), which is intriguing since the findspot is less than 1km from Rudge Hall (HE: 1189480) in the Rudge (or Rugge) parish of Shropshire. George, son of Sharington Talbot (1577-1642), was lord of the manor of Rudge in the early 17th century. When he passed away his widow remarried a Sir Clement Clarke and it was a descendent of theirs who sold the manor in 1714. It therefore seems likely that the vervel is associated with Sir John Talbot of Salwarp or his descendants.

Location: Shrewsbury Museum & Art Gallery.

D Thornton, P Reavill & I Richardson

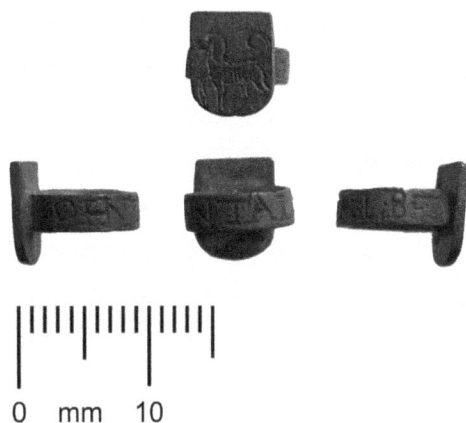

Vervel from Worfield (HESH-3A6AE5) (courtesy of the Portable Antiquities Scheme).

Cii04 SUFFOLK, THWAITE (PAS-EA634F; M&ME T109)

Date: c.1624-c.1685.

Description: Silver ring, circular in plan, and rectangular in section. Its flat exterior face is inscribed in semi-italic script: *King Charlles*. Attached horizontally to the ring, opposite the inscription is a shield-shaped plate. This is crudely engraved with the Royal Stuart arms: *quarterly, I and IV grandquarterly: 1 and 4, azure three fleurs de lys or (France modern) and 2 and 3 gules three lions passant guardant or (England); II or, a lion gules, double tressure*

flory and counter-flory of the same (Scotland); and III azure, a harp or, stringed argent (Ireland). Analysis at the British Museum produced a silver content of 97 percent. Ring: 9.17mm. Shield: 8.46mm x 7.84mm. 0.84g.

Discussion: This vervel is likely to be connected to either Charles I (r.1625-49) or (less likely) Charles II (r.1660-85). Thwaite Hall (HE: 1352532), which is very close to the findspot, was owned at this time by the Reeve (alias Wright) family (PLRG 2011); all that remains of the contemporary estate is a 17th century barn. Henry Reeve, a member of the royal Household, died of wounds suffered fighting for the King at the Battle of Edgehill (1642). His nephew, Sir George Reeve (c.1618-78) was elected an MP for Eye in 1660 and created a baronet in 1662. His father, Robert Reeve, had died around the same time as his uncle (HoP). In a 1636 petition by the rector of Thwaite to Archbishop Laud and the Commissioners for Causes Ecclesiastical for unpaid tithes, Robert Reeve was described as 'owner of great part of the parish, a man of contentious life and ill affected to the church' (CoSD: Charles I, 1636). Even with this known history, it is not known why this Royal vervel was found at Thwaite; maybe like **Ci10** this vervel belonged to a Royal hawk, rather than owned by the King in a personal capacity.

Location: The British Museum.

I Richardson & D Thornton

Vervel from Thwaite (PAS-EA634F) (courtesy of the Portable Antiquities Scheme).

CAROLVS DEI GRATIA MAGNÆ BRITANNIÆ FRANCIÆ ET HIBERN REX
Antonius Van Dyck Pinxit

King Charles I, engraving in the British Museum (© The Trustees of the British Museum).

Cii05 YORKSHIRE (EAST), SUTTON-UPON-DERWENT (YORYM-7576F7; 2012 T579)

Date: c.1550-c.1600.

Description: Silver ring, circular in plan, and of D-shaped section. Its flat exterior face is inscribed in serifed capital letters: {6-pointed star} F {triangle} VAGHAN. Attached horizontally to the ring is a shield-shaped plate, where the two ends join. The shield is engraved with a male head, with a snake wrapped around his throat. The snake's tail stands erect to the left of the male bust, and the snake's head is similarly erect to the right. Its tongue is in the form of an arrow pointing straight upwards. Ring: 8mm x 1.1mm. Shield: 9.5mm x 7.6mm. 1.2g.

Discussion: The crest upon the vervel is probably that of the Vaughan family of Sutton, East Yorkshire, who also had lands in Herefordshire and Wales: *a boy's head couped at the shoulders proper crined or, with a snake entwined about the neck vert* (Fairbairn 1905: 566).

The manor of Sutton-Upon-Derwent was granted by the Crown to John Dudley, Duke of Northumberland (1504-1553), in 1553, and in the same year it was transferred to John Eglesfield (d. 1566). Upon his death, Eglesfield bequeathed the parish to four gentleman, one of whom, Sir John Vaughan (c.1512-1577) – MP for Hedon, East Yorkshire in 1559, among many other constituencies between 1542-72 (HoP) – acquired two of the other shares by 1570 (BHO). John Vaughan's eldest son was Sir Francis Vaughan (1553-99), a candidate for the 'F Vaghan' named on the vervel (HoP). It is known that by the end of the 16th century, Francis owned the house of St Loys, probably the moated medieval manor house of the same name (HE: 1007818; BHO), and the vervel was found about 1km from this.

Location: Returned to finder/landowner; sold at Timeline Auctions (5/2/14; lot 0512).

I Richardson & R Griffiths

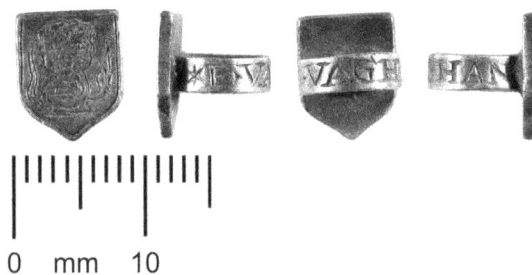

Vervel from Sutton-upon-Derwent (YORYM-7576F7) (courtesy of the Portable Antiquities Scheme).

Cii06 YORKSHIRE (NORTH), HUTTON CONYERS (DUR-775EF0; 2017 T329)

Date: c.1550-c.1650.

Description: Silver ring, circular in plan, and D-shaped in section. Its flat exterior face is inscribed S WYLL MMALL. Attached horizontally to the band, opposite the inscription, is a shield-shaped plate where the two ends of the ring join. This is engraved with a stylised horse's head resting on a torse. Ring: 9.68mm x 1.23mm. Shield: 9.97mm x 8.45mm x.1.41mm. 1.5g.

Discussion: The inscription upon this vervel probably identifies a Sir William Mallory. The crest of the family is given as a *nag's head, gules* (The Mallory Family 1905) and so is in keeping with the horse's head inscribed on this vervel. The Mallorys have been associated with the manor of Hutton Conyers through marriage into the Tempest and Conyers families from the 14th century onwards (BHO). The former site of Hutton Hall (HE: 1004074) is less than 1km from the vervel findspot.

William is a common family praenomen within this family. Sir William Mallory of Hutton Park and Studley (c.1525-1603) was member of Parliament for Yorkshire (1584) and Sheriff of Yorkshire (1592-3), and 'was very active in the suppression of Popery' (HoP). His Grandson, Sir William Mallory (1577/8-1646), was also an MP, but for Ripon (many times between 1614 and 1644), and an active royalist during the English Civil War, leaving the family with considerable debts and fines which 'whole estate both reall and personall would not extend by farr to satisfie' (HoP); indeed in his will he asked for his eldest son, John, also an MP, to pay off these debts (HoP). Either of these Williams may have been the original owner of the hawk which lost this vervel, however the style and form indicate that it was most likely associated with the latter Sir William Mallory.

Location: York Museums Trust.

B Westwood

Vervel from Hutton Conyers (DUR-775EF0) (courtesy of the Portable Antiquities Scheme).

Cii07 YORKSHIRE (NORTH), YORK area (BH-D703D3; 2007 T189)

Date: c.1600-c.1700.

Description: Silver ring, circular in plan, and of D-shaped section. Its flat exterior face is inscribed in serifed capital letters RAFE, between outward facing arrows. Attached horizontally to the ring, opposite the inscription, is a shield-shaped plate, attached at the point where the two parts of the ring join. This is engraved with a heraldic crest of a scallop shell (escallop) between two palm branches, wings or lobster claws resting on a torse. The base of the shield, which comes to a point, has been bent back over the ring. Ring: 10.47mm. Weight: 1.05g.

Discussion: Presumably the inscription on the ring indicates the first name of the owner, Rafe (Ralph), but could be the family name. Variations on the crest: *an escallop or, between two palm branches vert* can be attributed to a number of families, for example Aunsham, Awnsam (Fairbairn 1905: 24), Bustin (ibid, 91), Cenino (ibid, 106), etc., though not 'Rafe' or Ralph, according to the standard source.

The vervel was found prior to 1997, and only reported in 2007, with the result that its precise findspot is unknown. Without this information no further research into any of these possible family associations is possible.

Location: Returned to finder.

I Richardson & D Thornton

Vervel from York area (BH-D703D3) (courtesy of the Portable Antiquities Scheme).

Type Ciii: Shield-Shaped Plates with Ring Below

Ciii01 ESSEX, TOLLESHUNT MAJOR (SF-7E49A2; 2009 T761)

Date: c.1550-c.1650.

Description: Silver shield-shaped plate, above which is an integrally cast ring, circular in plan, and sub-rectangular in section. One face of the shield is inscribed in three rows of serifed capitals T/TYR/REL. A thin incised line traces the outline of the shield and another forms a groove in the centre of the ring. Ring: 5mm. Shield: 18.45mm x 9.07mm. 0.91g.

Discussion: According to one source, 'the family of Tyrell has always been celebrated in the history of this country, both on account of rank and influence, and the extent of their possessions'. These Tyrells were apparently descended from the Sir Walter Tyrell who accidentally killed King William II (r.1087-1100) (Wright 1836: 108-9). A string of Thomas Tyrells (or Tyrrells) from 'Heron' (now Herongate), Essex appear in the records from the early 15th century. Heronsgate is approximately 35km to the south west of the findspot. Sir Thomas Tyrell (d.1428) was the father of Elizabeth Tyrell (dates unknown), who married Sir Robert Darcy (c.1420-69), the brother of whom settled in Tolleshunt Darcy, the parish next to the one where the vervel was found (NA: PROB 11/7/329). The will of a later Sir Thomas Tyrrell (d.1477), shows that he owned manors in Tolleshunt Darcy at the time of his death (NA: PROB 11/6/417). A Thomas Tyrell of Heron is also recorded in the 1558 visitation of Essex (Metcalfe 1878). This may be the Thomas who was 18th in descent from Sir Walter and whose second son, another Thomas, had his seat in the manor of Ramsey Tyrell, Essex, near present day Ingotstone.

The closest surviving 16th or 17th century building to the findspot, is Beckingham Hall (HE: 1328223) which dates to 1543-6. This was in the possession of the Beckingham family from 1543 to 1636, when it was sold to Sir Thomas Adams (dates unknown). Stephen Beckingham (1550-1611) was married to an Avice (or Avis) Tyrell (dates unknown). A monument to the couple was formerly to be found in the nearby Church of St Nicholas (Kelly 1882). Given the number of Thomas Tyrells in the historical records, it is difficult to say which 'T' this might have belonged to, but the style of writing suggests a date prior to 1650.

Location: Returned to finder/landowner.

F Minter & I Richardson

Vervel from Tolleshunt Major (SF-7E49A2) (courtesy of the Portable Antiquities Scheme).

Ciii02 ESSEX, WITHAM area (ESS-D74C32; 2005 T529)

Date: c.1500-c.1550.

Description: Silver shield-shaped plate, above which is an integrally cast ring, oval in plan, and rectangular in section. One face of the shield is engraved with a lion rampant; traces of red enamel appear to survive in the lower right quadrant. The other face has the inscription in serifed capitals: T/NOR/FOC/K. Ring: 5.5mm. Overall: 20.8mm x 8.6mm. 1.28g.

Discussion: This vervel is very similar in form and in its decoration to that below (**Ciii02**). Both are roughly the same size as medieval harness pendants, though much lighter, and with an attachment loop more closely resembling that found on other vervels.

'T NORFOCK' and the coat of arms are probable references to the Dukes of Norfolk, whose family name is Howard. The 'T' could indicate the first name of the owner of the hawk which lost this vervel, several of whom bore the name Thomas. The Howard family experienced several changes of fortune in the 16th and 17th centuries. Thomas Howard, the 2nd Duke of Norfolk (1443-1524), was succeeded by his son, also called Thomas (1473-1554). Thomas, the 3rd Duke, was an influential member of Henry VIII's court until he fell out of favour in 1547; he was spared execution only by the King's death, and a subsequent pardon six years later by Queen Mary. His grandson, another Thomas Howard (1536-72), inherited the title of 4th Duke of Norfolk in 1554 and married Mary FitzAlan in the following year. Thomas was convicted of treason and executed for intriguing to have Mary Queen of Scots placed on the throne, with his property and titles declared forfeit. However, his and Mary's son, Philip Howard (1557-95), was able to inherit the Earldom of Arundel from his maternal grandfather in 1580, and this title was then passed to his son, Thomas Howard, 21st Earl of Arundel, 4th Earl of Surrey and latterly 1st Earl of Norfolk (1585-1646). The 21st Earl of Arundel was dubbed 'the Collector Earl' for his extensive art collection, compiled through trips to the Continent, and was close to both James I and Charles I. His grandson Thomas Howard (1627-77) became 5th Duke of Norfolk in 1660, when Charles II restored the title.

The arms on the vervel are almost colourless, but given the similarity to those on the vervel below (**Ciii03**) and the trace amount of what appears to be red enamelling, these could be interpreted as *gules, a lion rampant* and are likely either those of the FitzAlan Earls of Arundel (*gules, a lion rampant or*) or the Mowbray family (*gules, a lion rampant argent*). The former forms part of the coat of arms of the 4th and 5th Dukes, and the 1st Earl of Norfolk, while the latter features on the coat of arms of the 1st to 3rd Dukes.

The findspot is roughly 2km from Faulkbourne Hall (HE: 1337782), which was owned by the Fortescue family from 1494 until it was sold to Sir Edward Bullock in 1637. Henry VIII (1491-1547) is recorded as visiting Faulkborne several times in the 1520s. The vervel was also found around 10km north east of Beaulieu Palace, the surviving portion of which is now called New Hall (HE: 1338404), which in the early 16th century was sold by Thomas Boleyn (1477-1539) to Henry VIII. In 1527 Henry's court, including the 3rd Duke of Norfolk, spent more than a month at Beaulieu. Given the King's penchant for the hunt it is likely that much of this time was spent in the fields of this part of Essex, and it is tempting to think that the vervel was lost by the 3rd Duke, Thomas Howard (1473-1554), but this is purely conjecture.

Location: Braintree Museum.

I Richardson, P Reavill & C McDonald

Vervel from Witham area (ESS-D74C32) (courtesy of the Portable Antiquities Scheme).

Thomas Howard, 3rd Duke of Norfolk, engraving in the British Museum (© The Trustees of the British Museum).

Ciii03 HEREFORDSHIRE, SOUTH (HESH-A49557; 2007 T544)

Date: c.1500-c.1550.

Description: Silver shield-shaped plate, above which is an integrally cast ring, circular in plan, and rectangular in section. In profile the entire vervel is slightly bowed. One face of the plate is engraved with a lion rampant (*argent*) on a field of red enamel (*gules*), though areas of the red enamel have been lost from the upper parts of the shield; this shows that the face beneath has been deliberately roughened to serve as a key for the enamel. The other face has the inscription in serifed capitals: T / NOR/FOC/K; the letters regular, evenly spaced, and well cut, suggesting this is a well-made item. Ring: 5.5mm. Overall: 19.6mm x 10mm x 1.3mm. 1.31g

Discussion: The style and form of this vervel are virtually identical to those on **Ciii02**. It is therefore suggested that the likely owner is the same individual or one of their close relations.

Several grand houses are in the general area where the vervel was found. Roughly 1.2km south west of the findspot is the ruined Wilton Castle (HE: 1214349), home during the early post-medieval period to the Grey family. William Grey (1508/9-62), 13th Baron Grey of Wilton, was a commander in the English army under Henry VIII (1491-1547) and apparently had a rivalry with Henry Howard, Earl of Surrey (1516/17-47), son of the 3rd Duke of Norfolk. It therefore seems unlikely the Howard's were visiting the Grey's on their own accord.

About 1.3km from the findspot is Homme House (HE: 1099009), obtained by Thomas Kyrle (d.1577) in 1574. Kyrle had served as MP for Chichester in 1571; his son John (1568-1650) was later Sheriff of Herefordshire and a baronet (HoP). However, this place, or the family, has no obvious connections with the Howards.

Henry VIII also made a royal progress to the general area in 1535, with Anne Boleyn and members of his court, likely to include the Duke of Norfolk, passing as close to the findspot as Gloucester, where some of his time was spent hunting.

Location: Hereford Museum & Art Gallery.

P Reavill & I Richardson

Vervel from south Herefordshire (HESH-A49557) (courtesy of the Portable Antiquities Scheme).

Ciii04 HERTFORDSHIRE, LITTLE GADDESDEN
(BH-9487C5; 2004 T316)

Date: c.1550-c.1604.

Description: Silver shield-shaped plate, above which is an integrally cast ring, circular in plan (though distorted), and D-shaped in section. One face of the plate is engraved with the Royal Arms (as used by monarchs from the time of Edward III to Elizabeth I): *quarterly, first and fourth azure three fleurs-de-lis (two above and one below) or, second and third gules three lions passant guardant in a pale or*. The other face is engraved with a Tudor rose. There are signs of wear, indicating use, especially on one side of the ring (that with the Royal Arms). This object bears a resemblance to a vervel found in Colney, Norfolk (**Ciii05**) attributed to Charles Brandon, Duke of Suffolk (1484-1545), which suggests this is from a similar date. Ring: 11mm. Overall: 25.2mm x 14.2mm. 2.87g.

Discussion: This is the largest and heaviest vervel reported under the Treasure Act. It was found in 1985, but only reported in 2004; unfortunately, the result is that the only findspot information that survives is that it was discovered in the parish of Little Gaddesden, nothing more precise. A prominent historic property here is the early 19th century, neo-gothic, Ashbridge House (HE: 1348442), centrepiece of the Ashbridge Estate. An earlier iteration, Ashbridge Manor, was seized at the Dissolution of the Monasteries in 1538-9 with apparently Edward VI and Elizabeth spent much of their childhoods here (BHO). This may suggest that Henry VIII may have visited too; the inventory of

Henry VIII lists among his possessions 'IX vervells of silver with the kings armes' (MacGregor 2012).

Location: Returned to finder/landowner.

D Thornton & I Richardson

Vervel from Little Gaddesden (BH-9487C5) (courtesy of the Portable Antiquities Scheme).

King Henry VIII, engraving in the British Museum (© The Trustees of the British Museum).

Ciii05 NORFOLK, COLNEY (NMS-F2EEC6; 2013 T172)

Date: c.1514-c.1545.

Description: Silver shield-shaped plate, above which is an integrally cast ring, circular in plan, and circular in section. One face of the plate is inscribed with the royal arms as used from the time of Edward III to the end of the reign of Elizabeth I (as in **Ciii04**). The other face is inscribed with the arms of Charles Brandon, 1st Duke of Suffolk (1484-1545): *quarterly, first and fourth* (Brandon) *barry of ten argent and gules a lion rampant or ducally crowned per pale of the first and second, second and third* (Bruyn) *azure a millrind cross or (*Rokeby) *lozengy gules and ermine, quarterly*. There are traces of a light-coloured deposit in the fields of both shields which appears to represent the remains of gilding. Ring: 10mm. Overall: 23mm x 13mm x 1.5mm. 2.02g

Discussion: Charles Brandon was the son of Sir William Brandon (1456-1485), standard bearer for Henry VII (1457-1509), slain by Richard III (1452-85) in person at the Battle of Bosworth. He became Master of the Horse in 1513 and was created Duke of Suffolk in 1514. He married (without the King's permission) Mary Tudor, Henry VIII's sister, and widow of King Louis XII of France, in 1515.

The findspot is 7.5km west of Norwich, and not close to any of the major properties inhabited by the Duke of Suffolk. It therefore seems likely that either the vervel belonged to a bird that he brought with him on a visit to the city, or someone from the area was raising and/or training a bird that was owned by him. We know that on at least one occasion, when Charles Brandon returned from France in 1515, with his new wife Mary, he journeyed to Norwich, where he was 'well-received' (BHO).

Location: Norwich Castle Museum.

S Ashley & I Richardson

|||||||||||||||

0　mm　10

Vervel from Colney (NMS-F2EEC6) (courtesy of the Portable Antiquities Scheme).

Charles Brandon and Mary Tudor, engraving in the British Museum (© The Trustees of the British Museum).

Ciii06 NORFOLK, FOULSHAM (NMS-1E9786; 2007 T679)

Date: c.1558-c.1627.

Description: Silver shield-shaped plate, above which is an integrally cast ring, circular in plan, and rectangular in section. On the face of the plate is inscribed in italic script: *Fr Man / nock of / giffardes / hall*. The other face is inscribed: *in Stoke / in Suf. / esquire*. 17mm x 10mm x <1mm. 0.46g.

Discussion: The form of this item is different than most of the Ciii type vervels (above), as the attachment loop is very small (2.2mm diameter) and thin. It therefore seems unlikely to have been able to serve as point of attachment for a jess and leash. Clearly, though, it was intended to identify its owner and it could have been attached to a hunting bird or its equipment in another manner, so an association with falconry seems likely.

The inscription seems to refer to one of two men from the same family. Francis Mannock (1522-90) succeeded his father, William, at Gifford's Hall, Stoke by Nayland, Suffolk, in 1558. He married Mary, daughter of William Fitch of Canfield in Essex. He was buried at Nayland. His grandson, Sir Francis Mannock (1585-1634), 1st Baronet, succeeded his father William in 1616, and was created a baronet 1627. He and his father were both recusants.

Gifford's Hall (HE: 1283138) is approximately 100km south from the findspot of this item, so a long way away from where this vervel was lost. The closest grand house to the findspot, and which is old enough to be contemporary with the vervel, is Westfield House (HE: 1050988); this is about 1.4km from the findspot. No connection between that property and the Mannocks has been found.

Location: Norwich Castle Museum.

E Martin, S Ashley & E Darch

Vervel from Foulsham (NMS-1E9786) (courtesy of the Portable Antiquities Scheme).

Type D (Hinged Ring) Vervels

D01 SUSSEX (EAST), EAST HOATHLY WITH HALLAND (SUSS-F19E35; 2017 T969)

Date: c.1600-c.1700.

Description: Silver strip of rectangular section, forming a semi-circle in plan. At each end are two projecting sockets forming half of a hinge mechanism. The exterior face of the strip is inscribed in italic script: *Halland in Sussex.* 21.37mm x 4.59mm x 1.24mm. 1.53g.

Discussion: This example differs from the other vervels recorded in this catalogue (see introduction) as it appears to have been made in two parts to attach to the leg of the bird itself. Such vervels were described by early 17th century falconer Sir Thomas Sherley (1603), which he named 'garters'.

Although only half of this artefact was recovered, it is assumed that the diameter of the entire ring would have been c.21mm, making it almost twice the diameter of any of the other vervels recorded in this volume. The overall weight would also likely be in excess of 3g, which is also greater than the above cited examples. However, these dimensions are consistent with those of another vervel of this type in the collection of the British Museum (1913,0710.8). It is probable that both were intended to be used on larger birds, such as a female goshawk or eagle.

The vervel was found nearby to the former Halland House (HE: 1193327), an Elizabethan manor house built by Sir Thomas Pelham in 1595 but abandoned and dismantled after the death of the childless Thomas Pelham-Holles (1693-1768), 1st Duke of Newcastle-upon-Tyne and Prime Minister of Great Britain from 1754-56 and 1757-62. The ruins are still extant.

It seems likely, therefore, that this vervel relates to hawking activity by the Pelhams, or their ancestors or acquaintances, on this estate.

Location: Barbican House/Lewes Castle Museum hopes to acquire.

I Richardson

Type D vervel in the British Museum (1913,0710.8) (© The Trustees of the British Museum).

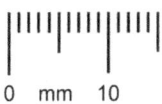

Vervel from East Hoathly with Halland (SUSS- F19E35) (courtesy of the Portable Antiquities Scheme).

Bibliography

Note: British History Online (BHO) is a great source for many local records, especially on parish history. Rather than reference these sources individually, readers are directed to the online corpus – https://british-history. ac.uk. This is also the case with the Oxford Dictionary of National Biography (DNB) – https://oxforddnb. com – and the History of Parliament (HoP) – https:// historyofparliamentonline.org – etc.

Adams, C. 2012. *Queen and Country: the significance of Elizabeth I's progress in Surrey, Sussex and Hampshire in 1591* (University of Southampton: unpublished PhD thesis).

Adelard of Bath. *Treatises on Birds* = Burnett, C. (ed.). 1998. *Adelard of Bath, Conversations with his Nephew: on the same and the different, questions on natural science, and on birds* (Cambridge: Cambridge University Press).

Anonymous. 1751. *The Parliamentary or Constitutional History of England; being a faithful account of all the most remarkable transactions in Parliament, from the earliest times to the Restoration of Charles II*, vol. 6, from the twenty-first year of James I to the second year of Charles I (London: Osborne & Sandby): https:// tinyurl.com/yc2g4myu.

Ashley, S. & Rogerson, A. 1997. 'Sir Robert Wynde's Hawk-Ring', *Norfolk Archaeology* 42, part 4, 538.

Bate, J. & Thornton, D. 2012. *Shakespeare: staging the world* (London: British Museum Press).

Bert, E. 1619. *An Approved Treatise on Hawkes and Hawking* (London: T.S).

BHO = British History Online: https://www.british-history.ac.uk.

Bonhams = Bonham auctioneers' sales (various, with sales date and lot number): https://bonhams.com.

Book of St Albans (1486) = Cambridge, University Library, Inc.3.J.4.1[3636]: https://cudl.lib.cam.ac.uk.

British Armorial Bindings. 2017 (Toronto: University of Toronto): https://armorial.library.utoronto.ca/stamp-owners/HER010.

Broadway, J. 2009. 'Agnes Throckmorton: a Jacobean recusant widow', in P. Marshall & G. Scott (eds.), *Catholic Gentry in English Society: the Throckmortons of Coughton from Reformation to Emancipation* (Farnham: Ashgate Publishing Ltd), 123-42.

Burke, B. 1884. *The General Armoury of England, Scotland, Ireland and Wales: comprising a registry of armorial bearings from the earlier to the present time* (London: Harrison & Sons).

Burke, J. & Burke, J. B. 1841. *A Genealogical and Heraldic History of the Extinct and Dormant Baronetcies of England, Ireland and Scotland* (London: Scott, Webster & Geary).

Burke, J. & Burke, J. B. 1844. *A Genealogical and Heraldic History of the Extinct and Dormant Baronetcies of England, Ireland and Scotland* (London: John Russell Smith).

Burke, J. & Burke, J. B. 1847. *A Genealogical and Heraldic Dictionary of the Landed Gentry of Great Britain and Ireland* (London: Henry Colburn).

CADW = National Historic Assets of Wales: https:// cadw.gov.wales/historicenvironment/recordsv1/cof-cymru/?lang=en.

CCP = Calendar of Cecil Papers in Hatfield House (various, with full reference after).

Chambers, J. 1829. *A General History of the County of Norfolk* (Norwich: John Stacy).

Chauncey, H. 1826. *The Historical Antiquities of Hertfordshire* (London: Griffin).

Cheesman, C. 2012. 'Artefacts of Interest Reported under the Portable Antiquities Scheme and the Treasure Act', *The Coat of Arms*, third series, vol. 8, part 1 (no. 223), 47-52.

Chesshyre, H. & Woodcock, T. 1992. *Dictionary of British Arms, Medieval Ordinary*, Volume 1 (London: Society of Antiquaries).

Christie, Manson & Woods 1855 = *Catalogue of the Celebrated Collection of Works of Art, from the Byzantine Period to that of Louis Seize, of that Distinguished Collector Ralph Bernal* (London: Christie, Manson & Woods): https://archive.org/details/christiceleb00chri.

Conservation Areas in East Dorset. 2006. *Horton*, East Dorset District Council Policy Planning Division, Supplementary Planning Guidance No.7 (April 2006).

Corder, J. 1965. *A Dictionary of Suffolk Arms* (Ipswich: Suffolk Record Office).

CoSD = Calendar of State Papers, Domestic (various, with full reference after).

CoSS = Calendar of State Papers, Scotland (various, with full reference after).

Cracrofts Peerage: https://www.cracroftspeerage.co.uk.

Cummings, J. 2001. *The Hound and the Hawk: the art of medieval hunting* (London: Phoenix Press).

Dalby, D. 1965. *Lexicon of the Medieval German Hunt: a lexicon of Middle High German Terms (1050-1500)* (Berlin: Gruyter).

D'Arcussia de Capré, C. 1615. *La fauconnerie de Charles d'Arcussia de Capré* (Paris: J. Houzé): https://gallica.bnf.fr/ark:/12148/btv1b8612032d/.

Diderot, D. & D'Alembert, J. 1751-72. *L'Encyclopédie* (Neûchatel: Inter-Livres).

DNB = *Oxford Dictionary of National Biographies*: https://www.oxforddnb.com.

Essex RO = Essex Record Office (various, with full reference after).

Evans, D. 1988. 'The Nobility of Knight and Falcon', in C. Harper-Bill & R. Harvey (eds.), *The Ideals and Practice of Medieval Knighthood* 3, Papers from the Fourth Strawberry Hill Conference (London: Boydell & Brewer), 79-100.

Fairbairn, J. 1905. *Fairbairn's Book of Crests of the Families of Great Britain and Ireland* (London: T. C. & E. C. Jack): https://archive.org/details/fairbairnsbookof01fair.

Frederick II. *De Arte Venandi cum Avibus* (the art of hunting with Birds) = Wood, C. A. & Fyfe, F. M. 1943. *De Arte cum Avibus* (Pasadena: Stanford University Press).

Furetière, A. 1690. *Dictionnaire universel* (The Hague & Rotterdam: Arnoud & Reinier Leers).

Gamister, D. & Margeson 1989 'A post-medieval silver hawking vervel', *Norfolk Archaeology* 11, part 3, 326-7.

Gentleman's Magazine 1795 = P.Q. 'Letters', *Gentleman's Magazine*, June 1795, 474.

Gibbons, A. 1898. *Notes on the Visitation of Lincolnshire 1634* (Lincoln: James Williamson): https://www.south-willingham.org/wp-content/uploads/2015/09/Notes-on-the-Visitation-of-Lincolnshire-1634-1898.pdf.

Glasier, P. 1998 (third edition). *Falconry and Hawking* (London: Batsford).

Grassby, R. 1997. 'The Decline of Falconry in Early Modern England', *Past & Present* 157 (November 1997), 37-62.

Griffiths, N. 1986. *Horse Harness Pendants*. Finds Research Group, Datasheet 5.

Hackett, R. R. 1899. *Wirksworth and Five Miles Round* (Wirksworth: F. W. Brooks).

Hartin, J. E. 1891. *Bibliotheca Acciptraria: a catalogue of books ancient and modern relating to falconry* (London: Bernard Quaritch).

HE = Historic England list of scheduled monuments and listed buildings in England: https://historicengland.org.uk/listing/the-list.

Herefordshire HER = Herefordshire Historic Environment Record (various, with full reference after).

Hill, G. 2004. *The Conquest of Ireland: a historical account of the plantation in Ulster at the commencement of the seventeenth century* (Kansas City: Irish Genealogical Foundation).

Hinde, W. 1857. *The Very Singular Life of John Bruen, Esquire, of Bruen Stapleford, Cheshire: exhibiting a variety of memorable and exemplary circumstances, which may be of great utility to all persons* (New York: E. O. Jenkins).

Hoare, C. M. 1918. *The History of an East Anglian Soke* (Bedford: Times Publishing Company).

HoC = House of Commons 1827. *A General Index to the First Fourteen Reports of the Commissioners Appointed to Inquire Concerning Charities in England and Wales* (London: House of Commons).

HoL = *Journal of the House of Lords*: https://www.british-history.ac.uk/lords-jrnl/.

HoP = The History of Parliament: https://www.historyofparliamentonline.org.

Hopkirk, M. 1934. *The Story of Layer de la Haye* (Colchester: Essex County Telegraph): https://retonheath.me.uk/history/mhopkirk.rtf.

Ivens, R. J. 1984. 'De Arte Venandi cum Avibus: an archaeological and historical introduction', *Cake and Cockhorse* (Magazine of the Banbury Historical Society), 9.5, 130-7.

Jackson, C. J. 1921. *English Goldsmiths and their Marks* (London: MacMillan and Co. Ltd.).

Jenkins, R. 1861. 'On the Gates of Bolougne, at Hardres Court, Upper Hardres', *Archaeologia Cantiana* 4: https://kentarchaeology.org.uk/Research/Pub/ArchCant/004-1861/004-03.pdf.

Kelly, E.R. 1882. *Kelly's Directory of Essex.* (London: Kelly & Co.).

Land and Use Co. 2018. *North Norfolk Landscape Character Assessment.* See: https://north-norfolk.gov.uk/media/4720/north-norfolk-landscape-character-assessment-2018-final-draft-spd.pdf.

Landau, G. 1849. *Beiträge zur Geschichte der Jagd und der Falknerei in Deutschland* (Kassel: Theodor Fischer).

Latham, S, 1614, *Lathams Falconry: or The Faulcons Lure, and Cure: in two books* (London: Roger Jackson – made available from the Henry F Huntington Library & Art Gallery).

Lewis, M. J. 2007. 'Identity and Status in the Bayeux Tapestry: the iconographic and artefactual evidence',

Anglo-Norman Studies 29 (Woodbridge: Boydell), 100-20.

Lewis, M. J. (ed.). 2012. 'Report of the Portable Antiquities Scheme 2011', *Post Medieval Archaeology* 46, Part 2, 320-32.

Lewis, M. J. 2016. 'A Detectorist's Utopia? Archaeology and Metal-Detecting in England and Wales', *Open Archaeology* 2, 127-39.

Lewis, M. & Richardson, I. 2017. 'Inscribed Vervels', *Post Medieval Archaeology* 51/1, 194-200.

Lewis, M. & Speakman, N. 2016. *Los Pilares de Europa: la edad media en el British Museum* (Barcelona: Obra Social la Caixa).

MacGregor, A. 2012. *Animal Encounters: human and animal Interaction in Britain from the Norman Conquest to World War I* (London: Reaktion Books).

MacLeod, C. & Wilks, T. 2013. *The Lost Prince: the life and death of Henry Stuart* (London: National Portrait Gallery).

Maddison, A. R. 1891. *Lincolnshire Wills: second series AD 1600-1617* (Lincoln: James Williamson).

Margeson, S. 1994 'Clement Pastor's hawk ring', *Norfolk Archaeology*, 42, 538.

Metcalfe, W. 1878. *The Visitations of Essex* (London: Mitchell & Hughes): https://archive.org/stream/visitationsesse00britgoog/visitationsesse00britgoog_djvu.txt.

Monks in Motion. Durham University research project: https://dur.ac.uk/mim/about/.

Morel, P. & Horobin, D. 2018. *Hawks' varvels* (Milton Keynes: Lightening Source).

NA = National Archives (various, with full reference after).

Nichols, J. 1828. *The Progresses, Processions, and Magnificent Festivities of King James the First, His Royal Consort, Family and Court* 4 (London: Society of Antiquaries of London).

Norfolk HER = Norfolk Historic Environment Record (various, with full reference after).

Oggins, R. S. 2004. *The Kings and their Hawks* (New Haven & London: Yale University Press).

Oggins, V. D. and Oggins, R. S. 1992. 'Hawkers and Falconers along the Ouse: A Geographic Principle of Location in some Serjeanty and Related Holdings', *Proceedings of the Cambridge Antiquarian Society* 80, 7-20.

O'Laughlin, M. C. 2001. *The Families of County Donegal, Ireland* (Kansas: Irish Genealogical Foundation).

Oman, C. 1974. *British Rings* (London: Batsford).

Parker, J. 1894. *A Glossary of Terms Used in Heraldry* (London & Oxford: James Parker & Co).

Pentin, H. 1906. 'Title'. *Proceedings. Dorset Natural History and Archaeological Society* (Dorchester: Dorset County Chronicle).

Pitt, W. 1817. *A Topographical History of Staffordshire: including its agriculture, mines and manufactures...* (Newcastle-under-Lyme: J Smith).

PLRG. 2011. Historical Record of the Parish Church of St George: https://thwaite.onesuffolk.net.

Robbins, K. 2014. *Portable Antiquities Scheme: A Guide for Researchers* (London: British Museum): https://finds.org.uk/research/advice.

Robinson, J. M. 2017. 'The Magnificent Puzzle of Crichel; one of Dorset's grandest Georgian houses, *Country Life Magazine*, February 2017: https://countrylife.co.uk/country-life/the-magnificent-puzzle-of-crichel-one-of-dorsets-grandest-georgian-houses-149761.

Rye, W. 1913. *Norfolk Families* (Norwich: Goose and Son, Ltd).

Schelgel, H. & Wilverhorst, J. A. V. 1853. *Traité de Fauconnerie* (Leide: Institut Lithographique, Arnz et Comp).

Sherley, T. 1603 (2004 edition). *A Short Discourse of Hawking to the Field* (Boise: The Peregrine Fund).

Shropshire Archives (various, with full reference after).

Sil, N. P. 2001. *Tudor Placemen and Statesmen: select case histories* (Vancouver: Farleigh Dickinson University Press).

Spokes, P. S. 1938. 'Coats of Arms in Berkshire Churches', *Berkshire Archaeological Journal* 42, 29-66.

Strong, R. 2000. *Henry, Prince of Wales and England's Lost Renaissance* (London: Pimlico).

Suffolk HER = Suffolk Historic Environment Record (various, with full reference after).

The Mallory Family. 1905. *The Virginia Magazine of History and Biography*, 13 (2), 216-19: http://jstor.org/stable/4242740.

Thomson, G. S. 1940. *Life in a Noble Household 1641-1700* (London: Jonathan Cape).

Turberville, G. 1611. *The Book of Faulconrie or Hawking* (London: Thomas Purfoot).

Vincent, T. H. 1994. 'Heur et malheur de la vervelle à faucon ou l'erreur de Schlegel et Wulverhorst', in C. Parpoil & T Vincent (eds.), *La chasse au vol fil des temps* (Glen: Musée International de la Chasse), 72-94.

Warwickshire CR = Warwickshire County Record Office archives (various, with full reference after).

Waters, R. E. C. 1878. *Genealogical Memoirs of the Extinct Family of Chester of Chicheley, their Ancestors and Descendants* (London: Robson & Sons).

Webster, L. 2012. *Anglo-Saxon Art* (London: British Museum).

Westcote, T. 1845. *A View of Devonshire in MDCXXX with a Pedigree of Most of its Gentry* (Exeter: William Roberts).

Wigley, D. A. 1965. 'Some Notes on the Wigley Family of Derbyshire', *Derbyshire Miscellany, Bulletin* 3 (Derbyshire Archaeological Society), 579-87.

Winchester City Council. 2004. *Landscape Character Assessment: Winchester District.* https://winchester.gov.uk/planning/landscape---countryside/landscape-character-assessment/.

Wiveton Hall History. 2018: see http://wivetonhall.co.uk/history.

Wright, T. 1836. *The History and Topography of the County of Essex* (London: George Virtue).

Appendix A

Potential Vervels

A number of small items have been recorded with the Portable Antiquities Scheme and identified as potential vervels. All but one of these are not inscribed with text or a heraldic image, and therefore do not serve the purpose (necessary of a vervel) – to identify the owner of the bird. They are more likely to be finger-rings, although small in size. The exception, **X05**, is a small heraldic plate, though there is no evidence of whether or how this might have been attached to a raptor or its jess.

X01 CUMBRIA, BURTON IN KENDALL
(LVPL2271; 2002 T205)

Date: c.1400-c.1600.

Description: Silver ring or band, circular in plan, and rectangular in section; the band is now split. Its exterior face is decorated with a carved 'tooth pattern' border, and a pair of diagonal bands with carved pattern, and a star with dot in the fields between the bands. 18mm. 5.34g.

Discussion: The weight of this object seems too heavy for a vervel, so it could well be a finger ring.

Location: Returned to finder/landowner.

N Herepath

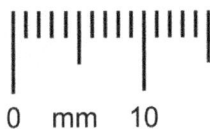

Ring from Burton in Kendall (LVPL2271) (courtesy of the Portable Antiquities Scheme).

X02 CUMBRIA, KENDALL (LANCUM-327EA0)

Date: c.1500-c.1700.

Description: Gilded copper-alloy ring, consisting of an intact base ring, to which two thinner rings, of broadly similar form, were applied at the top and bottom; one is coming loose. The base ring is circular in plan, and rectangular in section, and decorated with a floral ornament; a repetitive pattern of a flower with stalk, petals and leaves. The outer rings are circular in plan, and semi-circular in section, and have upon them moulded criss-cross decoration with traces of gilding left inside. The internal face is smooth and undecorated. 17mm x 9mm x 1mm. 3.9g.

Discussion: It has been suggested that this object is a vervel, but more likely a post-medieval finger ring, perhaps for a child. A very similar example has been recorded from Wellington, Herefordshire (WAW-6FDC67), though the Kendall example is much larger.

Location: Returned to finder/landowner.

D Boughton

X03 HAMPSHIRE, DAMERHAM (WILT-7B06C5)

Date: c.1400-c.1700.

Description: Copper-alloy plate of sheet metal, rolled so that the two ends almost touch to form a ring, circular in plan and rectangular in section. The outside of the ring is decorated with v-shaped punches around its circumference. The ring varies in width and the two ends have v-shaped notches in them. 17.5mm x 1mm.

Discussion: This could be a piece of metal that was applied to a larger object, and is unlikely to be a vervel.

Location: Returned to finder/landowner.

K Hinds

X04 HEREFORDSHIRE, LUDLOW area
(HESH-70C2E2)

Date: c.1800-c.1900.

Description: Cast copper-alloy ring, circular in plan, and broadly rectangular in section with a recessed exterior face and knops present around the edge. The exterior face has the inscription, in capital letters .REGARD FOR GE: IV – probably identifying King George IV (r. 1820-30). 16.8mm x 7.7mm x 1.8mm. 3.1g.

Discussion: This object is quite heavy for a vervel, and more likely to be a finger ring.

Location: Returned to finder/landowner.

P Reavill

X05 HEREFORDSHIRE, WELLINGTON (WAW-6FDC67)

Date: c.1600-c.1700.

Description: Gilded copper-alloy ring, circular in plan, and broadly rectangular in section with a recessed exterior face and raised moulded decoration (top and bottom) on the edges. The decoration consists of a double row of conjoined pellets. The middle of the ring is plain apart from some traces of gilding surviving. A square point cut translucent yellow stone has been applied to the middle section of the ring. It is probable that this stone is cut glass, but it is also possible that it could be a yellow semi-precious stone such as citrine. The internal face is smooth and undecorated. 11.60mm x 5.11mm x 1.31mm. 1.1g.

Discussion: This object, though recorded as a potential vervel, is almost certainly a finger ring; no recorded vervels incorporate jewels or gems.

Location: Returned to finder/landowner.

T Gilmore & P Reavill

Ring from Wellington (WAW-6FDC67) (courtesy of the Portable Antiquities Scheme).

X06 KENT, SWINGFIELD (KENT-7D70EC)

Date: c.1500-c.1700.

Description: Copper-alloy ring gilded, circular in plan and roughly D-shaped in section. The exterior face is decorated with two parallel lines of beading running around the central circumference of the ring. The copper-alloy metal shows through dark brown where the gilding has worn off, dark green where the copper has patinated, and light and green where verdigris is corroding through the golden gilding. 14.91mm x 7.13mm x 1.81mm. 2.06g.

Discussion: This is also simply a small ring, lacking any means by which the owner would be identified.

Location: Returned to finder.

J Ahmet & I Richardson

X07 KENT, TENTERDEN (SUSS-79D987; 2016 T270)

Date: c.1500-c.1800.

Description: Silver ring, circular in plan and D-shaped in section. The outer surface is decorated with a raised repeating pelleted pattern around the circumference with a bevelled band on either side. The internal surface of the ring is smooth and undecorated. 11.4mm x 3.9mm x 1mm. 0.78g

Discussion: This was presumably thought to be a vervel because of its small size, but with no means to identify the owner, it is simply a small ring.

Location: Returned to the finder/landowner.

L Walker & I Richardson

X08 KENT, WINCHEAP (KENT-D47900)

Date: c.1500-c.1800.

Description: Copper-alloy ring of rectangular section and circular in plan. It has two bands of a moulded foliate design, each one bordering the upper and lower circumference. The ring is decorated with a series of eight, six-pointed star cut-outs, which are evenly spaced around the ring creating an openwork design. The ring is covered with regular arrangement of very small raised dots and there are small traces of gilding covering the entire object. There is a raised '8' on the ring, between two of the openwork stars. The internal surface of the ring is smooth and undecorated.

Discussion: The lack of an inscription on this object suggests it did not function as a vervel.

Location: Returned to the finder/landowner.

C Chestnutt

X09 LEICESTERSHIRE, GREAT EASTON
(RAH1147)

Date: c.1300-c.1600.

Description: Gold ring, ovoid in plan and rectangular in section. There appears to be piece of applied decoration on the outer face. 14.85mm x 3.93mm x 0.95mm. 1.18g.

Discussion: This item was reportedly found in 1996, prior to the implementation of the Treasure Act, and the existing record is very scant. The only photograph shows the ring from above, so it is not possible to say whether there is an inscription or other feature which would allow the owner to be identified. Efforts to speak with the original finder have so far been unsuccessful.

Location: Returned to the finder/landowner.

R Harte & I Richardson

X10 LINCOLNSHIRE, SPILSBY (LIN-38F05B, 2017 T831)

Date: c.1370-c.1410.

Description: Silver-gilt fragment of a plate, sub-rectangular in plan. Three of the sides are straight and the fourth is broken in a jagged line. Each face of the fragment is decorated with a coat-of-arms; one on face is the right half of a silver cross with frilled edges in the top and bottom, gilded quarters with the possible remains of niello in the frills, all within an incised line border. The reverse of the object has been decorated with an incised pattern within an incised line border, depicting two lions rampant-couchant. 16.89mm x 8.98mm x 1.76mm. 1.87g.

Discussion: The arms on one side appear to be associated with the Willoughby family, specifically William Willoughby, 5th Baron Willoughby de Erseby (c.1370-1409); *sable, a cross engrailed or*, though his son, the 6th Baron (c.1385-1452) also had the same arms. The 5th Baron remained loyal to King Henry IV (r. 1399-1413) during the uprising of Henry Hotspur, and his son fought for Henry V (r. 1413-22) at Harfleur and Agincourt (both 1415) during the Hundred Years War. The remains of Eresby Hall (HE: 1020032) are on the site of the former medieval manor of Eresby, and are less than 200m from the findspot of this item.

The small size and heraldic nature of this object have led to conjecture that it is a vervel, though without any sign of a ring or form of attachment, that remains speculative.

Location: Returned to finder/landowner.

S Burford & I Richardson

Plate from Spilsby (LIN-38F05B) (courtesy of the Portable Antiquities Scheme).

X11 SHROPSHIRE, ERCALL (HESH-0E91D3)

Date: c 1600-c.1800.

Description: Cast copper-alloy ring, circular in plan, and broadly D-shaped in section with a raised central ridge flanked by two grooves, which are in turn flanked by large ridges with small projecting decorative knops projecting; these appear to depict flowers and leaves. The internal face is flat and plain. The metal is a mid-green colour with active corrosion present beneath. 13.7mm x 5.3mm x 1.5mm. 1.46g.

Discussion: Recorded as a possible vervel, this is almost certainly a finger-ring.

Location: Returned to finder/landowner.

P Reavill

Ring from Ercall (HESH-0E91D3) (courtesy of the Portable Antiquities Scheme).

X12 SHROPSHIRE, OSWESTRY (HESH-EAD622)

Date: c.1650-c.1800.

Description: Lead-alloy ring, circular in plan and D-shaped in section. The external face is decorated with a simple geometric pattern comprising interlocking lozenges (joined horizontally by their points) contained within two circumferential raised bands that border the upper and lower edges. 13.8mm x 4.2mm x 1.0mm. 1.06g

Discussion: This object is of similar size and weight to many vervels, but lacking any means of identifying the owner, probably is not one. Lead is also an unlikely metal to have been used to make a vervel.

Location: Returned to finder/landowner.

P Reavill

X13 STAFFORDSHIRE, COPENHALL
(WMID-163E47)

Date: c.1400-c.1700.

Description: Cast copper-alloy ring, circular in plan and broadly rectangular in section. Its exterior face has an openwork design of alternately pointing triangles set between two collars. Between the triangles there is a moulded background of tiny pellets. 13.72mm x 6.42mm x 1.57mm.1.3g.

Discussion: Due to the small size of the ring it has been suggested that it functions as a vervel, but this is less likely in this case.

Location: Returned to finder/landowner.

T Brindle

Ring from Copenhall (WMID-163E47) (courtesy of the Portable Antiquities Scheme).

X14 SUSSEX (EAST), FIRLE (SUSS-9626E3)

Date: c.1600-c.1700.

Description: Copper-alloy ring, circular in plan, and broadly rectangular in section, with traces of gilding surviving on the surface. The external face of the ring is decorated with two parallel bands of lines, with an engraved ropework border on either edge of the ring. The surface is abraded. 14.2mm x 3.8mm x 0.9mm. 0.89g.

Discussion: This ring is similar to a Type B vervel in form, but of copper-alloy. A vervel in the British Museum, of similar form, is inscribed 'of Rushbrooke in Suf[folk]' (MLA 1856,8-27,109; Gaimster & Margeson 1989: 324-5). Nonetheless, this is unlikely to be a vervel.

Location: Returned to finder/landowner.

L Andrews-Wilson

X15 WILTSHIRE, WEST LAVINGTON
(WILT-A91A20)

Date: c.1400-c.1700.

Description: Copper-alloy ring of unknown section, presumably circular in plan. The outer face is decorated along the central band in a series of ovals.

Discussion: There is no photograph of this object, but given that it does not attempt to identify its owner, it is very unlikely to be a vervel.

Location: Returned to finder/landowner.

K Hinds

X16 WILTSHIRE, WINTERBOURNE
(WILT-F3D203)

Date: c.1500-c.1700.

Description: Copper-alloy ring, seemingly circular in plan, and rectangular in section. The object appears to have been cast in two C-shaped pieces, which have then been joined together. One join has straight edges and is a little off-kilter, whilst the other has very rough edges and suggests a break and/or repair. The interior face is smooth and shows no sign of either join. Perhaps this indicates the joins are actually casting seams. The exterior face of the object is decorated with elongated lozenges, long point to long point, the shorter points touching the rim that runs around each edge. These create triangular shapes to each side, which slant downwards and outwards, giving the outer face a faceted appearance. The exterior face has a dark brown patina, whilst its interior face has traces of a white residue. 12.5mm x 0.5mm.

Discussion: There is no photo of this object.

Location: Returned to finder/landowner.

K Hinds

X17 YORKSHIRE (NORTH), KIRKBY FLEETHAM WITH FENCOTE (YORYM-6560D7)

Date: c.1600-c.1700.

Description: Cast copper-alloy ring, circular in plan, and broadly rectangular in section. It is decorated with a series of incised lines and five evenly spaced lozenge shapes within a raised border of conjoined lozenges. Traces of gilding are present on the outer face. The internal face of the ring is flat and undecorated. The metal is a dark blackish-brown colour and is worn. 16.3mm x 5.9mm x 1.3mm. 1.8g.

Discussion: Similar examples of this object can be seen above.

Location: Returned to finder/landowner.

R Griffiths

X18 YORKSHIRE (WEST), WOLVEY (LEIC-1F5D16; 2014 T304)

Date: c.1400-c.1700.

Description: Silver ring of rectangular section, forming an incomplete circle in plan. The outer surface is decorated in a series of five incised X's. Attached to the outer face is a sub-rectangular bezel/attachment which is divided into four quadrants by linear depressions radiating from the centre, giving the impression of a clover leaf. 14mm x 4mm x 1mm. 0.88g

Discussion: This was thought to possibly be a vervel on account of its size, but there is no evidence that it could have been used to identify its owner. It is more likely a small finger-ring.

Location: Returned to finder/landowner.

W Scott

X19 UNKNOWN FINDSPOT (WMID-9DD75C)

Date: c.1600-c.1800.

Description: Copper-alloy ring, circular in plan and D-shaped in section. The outer face is decorated with a repeating scroll design. 14.1mm x 3.5mm x 2.3mm. 1.62g.

Discussion: Another example likely to simply be a small ring.

Location: Returned to finder/landowner.

V Allnatt

Appendix B

Vervels in Museums (not otherwise catalogued above)

Most of these vervels do not have known findspots, and indeed it is possible that some were never lost but instead passed through various hands over the centuries before they were acquired by museums.

Type A

BEDFORDSHIRE, BIGGLESWADE (unknown date of discovery)

Date: c.1399-c.1413.

Description: Gold flat circular ring, rectangular in section, inscribed on one in black-letter script face: *sum* {four-pointed star} *regis* {four-pointed star} *anglie* {flourish} and on the other: *St* {four-pointed star} *comitis* {four-pointed star} *herfordie* {four-pointed star}. It is unclear if the 'St' is meant to be read as 'et' or whether it is actually just another decorative element. 16.2mm x 1mm. 2.9g.

Discussion: This is the only confirmed extant gold vervel in a public collection in Britain. The subject is thought to be Henry IV (r.1399-1413) who was created Earl of Hereford in 1384.

Location: British Museum (1855,1201.217).

LINCOLNSHIRE, GAINSBOROUGH (unknown date of discovery)

Date: c.1610-c.1643.

Description: Silver flat circular ring, rectangular in section, inscribed on both faces in italic script: *Sir William // Constable* {three five-pointed stars}. Dimensions not recorded.

Discussion: Sir William Constable, 1st Baronet (1590-1655), served the Parliamentarian cause in the English Civil War and was present at the siege of Gainsborough (December 1643), which may explain this vervel's loss in the area.

Location: North Lincolnshire Museum.

NORFOLK, ASHILL (found 1993)

Date: c.1500-c.1600.

Description: Silver flat circular ring, rectangular in section, inscribed on one face in italic script: *Clement. Paston. Esq. of.* 11mm x 1mm. 0.83g.

Location: Norwich Castle Museum (1993.13).

NORFOLK, HARLING (found 1978)

Date: c.1600-c.1700.

Description: Silver flat circular ring, rectangular in section, inscribed on one face in italic script: {cross} *Garboldishm. Norff.* 14mm x 1mm. 1.63g.

Location: Norwich Castle Museum (1978.422).

UNKNOWN FINDSPOT or DATE of DISCOVERY

Date: c.1643-c.1646.

Description: Silver flat circular ring, rectangular in section, inscribed on one face in italic script: *Couronell • Hutchinson ⸓.* 0.3g.

Location: V&A Museum (M.143.1984).

UNKNOWN FINDSPOT or DATE of DISCOVERY

Date: c.1643-c.1646.

Description: Silver flat circular ring, rectangular in section, inscribed on one face in italic script: *Gouern. of. Nottingham* {star}. 0.7g.

Discussion: Almost certainly one of a pair, along with the vervel above. Col. John Hutchinson (1615-64) was a Roundhead and Governor of Nottingham Castle (1643-6).

Location: V&A Museum (M.143.A.1984).

UNKNOWN FINDSPOT or DATE of DISCOVERY

Date: c.1600-c.1700.

Description: Silver flat circular ring, rectangular in section, inscribed on one face in italic script: *of Rushbrooke in Suf.* 0.46g.

Location: British Museum (1856,0627.109).

Type B

UNKNOWN FINDSPOT or DATE of DISCOVERY

Date: c.1600-c.1633.

Description: Silver ring, circular in plan and D-shaped in section. Inscribed in italics on the flat exterior face: *S Henry Lee K baroet.* 0.3g.

Discussion: Probably associated with Sir Henry Lee (d.1633), 1st Baronet, who inherited Ditchley House from his cousin, another Sir Henry Lee (1533-1611). The style of script on this vervel is identical to that on the vervel below, and the two are very likely to be associated.

Location: V&A Museum (M.143.D.1984b).

UNKNOWN FINDSPOT or DATE of DISCOVERY

Date: c.1600-c.1633.

Description: Silver ring, circular in plan and D-shaped in section. Inscribed in italics on the flat exterior face: *of Ditchley neare Oxd:* 0.4g.

Discussion: The message on this vervel compliments that on the vervel above, and the two are very likely to be associated.

Location: V&A Museum (M.143.B.1984).

Type Ci

UNKNOWN FINDSPOT or DATE of DISCOVERY

Date: c.1600-c.1650.

Description: Silver ring, circular in plan and D-shaped in section. The flat exterior face inscribed in italics: *Sponsor* followed by a foliate flourish. Opposite the inscription, where the two ends of the ring meet, a shield-shaped plate is attached vertically with solder. The face of the plate is engraved with a heraldic crest showing a flaming beacon. 0.8g.

Discussion: Possibly connected to Spencer Compton, 2nd Earl of Northampton (1601-43), whose crest is listed as *on a wreath a beacon, sable, enflamed on the top, proper.*

Location: V&A Museum (M.143.C.1984).

UNKNOWN FINDSPOT or DATE of DISCOVERY

Date: c.1500-c.1600.

Description: Silver ring, circular in plan and D-shaped in section. The flat exterior face inscribed in serifed capitals: {*five-pointed* star} BOURBON. Opposite the inscription a small shield-shaped plated is attached vertically. The face of the shield is decorated with the arms of the Duke of Bourbon. White enamelling remains in the letters of the inscription and on the shield. Unknown dimensions.

Discussion: The Dukes of Bourbon were prominent in the French nobility. In 1531 the Duchy merged with the other titles held by the monarchy for the first time.

Location: British Museum (OA.9197; AF.336).

UNKNOWN FINDSPOT or DATE of DISCOVERY

Date: c.1600-c.1700.

Description: Silver ring circular in plan and D-shaped in section. The flat exterior face inscribed in semi-italics: *Mr Richard Cope of.* Opposite the inscription a shield-shaped plate is attached vertically to the ring. The outside face of the shield are engraved a wolf-headed fleur-de-lis on a

mount (the arms of Cope). Shield: 10.85mm x 8.04mm. 1.16g.

Location: British Museum (OA.9198; AF.337).

UNKNOWN FINDSPOT or DATE of DISCOVERY

Date: c.1627-c.1640.

Description: Silver ring, circular in plan and D-shaped in section. The flat exterior face inscribed in italics: *Will Sherard•of.* Opposite the inscription a shield-shaped plate is attached vertically to the ring. The exterior face of the shield is engraved with a coat-of-arms: a chevron between three balls. These are the arms of Sherard: *Argent a chevron gules between three torteaux.* Ring: 9.1mm. Shield: 8.9mm. 1.11g.

Discussion: Sir William Sherard (1588-1640) of Stapleford, Leicestershire was elevated to the peerage and created Baron of Leitrim in 1627. He is buried in church of St Mary Magdalene, Stapleford. It is very similar in shape, size and content to the vervel below, differing only in the inscription and the shape of the shield (which in this case is more kite-like). However, the two do not appear to complement on another, and presumably would have been used on different birds.

Location: British Museum (1927,0216.68).

UNKNOWN FINDSPOT or DATE of DISCOVERY

Date: c.1627-c.1640.

Description: Silver ring, circular in plan and D-shaped in section. The flat exterior face inscribed in italics: *Will lord Sherard.* Opposite the inscription, a shield-shaped plate is attached vertically to the ring. The exterior face of the shield is engraved with a coat-of-arms: a chevron between three balls. These are the arms of Sherard: *Argent a chevron gules between three torteaux.* Ring: 9.1mm. Shield: 8.9mm (length). 0.89g.

Discussion: See vervel above.

Location: British Museum (1927,0216.68).

Type Cii

UNKNOWN FINDSPOT or DATE of DISCOVERY

Date: c.1493-c.1567.

Description: Silver ring, circular in plan and of rectangular section. The ring is uninscribed. A shield-shaped plate is attached horizontally. The face of the plate is gilded and coloured with the arms of the Anne, Duc de Montmorency (1493-1567) *or, a cross gules, between sixteen alerions azure.* 32mm x 30mm x 8mm.

Discussion: This vervel is larger than all of the catalogued examples from England and Wales (above), and closer in size to a typical harness pendant. However, the presence of the ring on the reserve of the plate suggests that it is indeed a vervel, though probably one for quite a large bird.

The Duke of Montmorency was an important figure in 16th century France, serving as a soldier and statesman for most of his adult life.

Location: Kunsthistorisches Museum, Vienna (Hofjagd- und Rustkammer, D50).

UNKNOWN FINDSPOT or DATE of DISCOVERY

Date: c.1640-c.1703.

Description: Silver ring, circular in plan and D-shaped in section. On the flat exterior face, absent any inscription, a shield-shaped plate is attached horizontally to the ring. The exterior face of the shield is engraved with a coat-of-arms: three birds on a bend. These are the likely the arms of Degge: *Or, on a bend azure three falcons rising argent, jessed and belled of the first* (Burke 1884: 273). Ring: 9.65mm. Shield: 8.4mm. 0.97g.

Discussion: The Museum's catalogue description suggests this vervel might belong to Sir Simon Degge (1612-1703) who was High Sherriff of Derbyshire in 1675.

Location: British Museum (1927,0216.69).

Type D

UNKNOWN FINDSPOT or DATE of DISCOVERY

Date: c.1620-1660.

Description: Silver ring, circular in plan and D-shaped in section. It appears to consist of two interlocking hemispheres that are connected by a hinge on one end and a locking bezel on the other. The flat exterior face is inscribed in italics: *Iohn Couentrey Esqr. in Worcestershire*. The bezel is engraved with the Coventry coat-of-arms: *Sable a fess ermine between three crescents or*. Crest: *A garb lying fessways or, thereupon a cock gules combed, wattled and legged gold* (Burke 1884: 235). 20.15mm. 4.07g.

Discussion: It is possible this vervel is associated with John Coventry (d.1652) who served as MP for Evesham in 1641-42. His son, another John (c.1636-1685) was knighted in 1660, so if the vervel was his, it would likely predate this event. This is only one of two 'Type D' vervels known, the other is entry **D01** in the catalogue above.

Location: British Museum (1913,0710.8).

Appendix C

Vervels in Private Collections (not otherwise catalogued above)

Type A

SUFFOLK, BECCLES (found 1980)

Date: c.1600-c.1700.

Description: Silver flat circular ring, rectangular in section. Inscribed on one face in italic script: *Santon Downham in Suff.* 12mm. 0.29g.

Location: Sold at *Timeline Auctions* 15-16 March 2012, Lot 111?

UNKNOWN FINDSPOT or DATE of DISCOVERY

Date: c.1600-c.1700.

Description: Silver flat circular ring, rectangular in section. Inscribed on one face in italic script: *Borton upon. Dvnsmore.* 16mm. 1.3g.

Location: Sold at *Timeline Auctions* 15 March 2013, Lot 981.

UNKNOWN FINDSPOT or DATE of DISCOVERY

Date: c.1600-c.1700.

Description: Silver flat circular ring, rectangular in section. Inscribed on both faces in italic script: {8-pointed star} *Sir John* {cross} *Clopton* {2x 8-pointed star}// {8-pointed star} *of Warwickshyre.* 14mm. 1.07g.

Location: Sold at *Timeline Auctions* 9-12 September 2015, Lot 889.

UNKNOWN FINDSPOT or DATE of DISCOVERY

Date: c.1600-c.1700.

Description: Silver flat circular ring, rectangular in section. Inscribed on both faces in italic script: *Att. Castle. Camps* {six-pointed star} // {six-pointed star} *In. Cambridgeshear.* 12mm. 0.52g.

Location: Sold at *Timeline Auctions* 30 August – 3 September 2016, Lot 2505.

UNKNOWN FINDSPOT or DATE of DISCOVERY

Date: c.1600-c.1700.

Description: Silver flat circular ring, rectangular in section. Inscribed on both faces in italic script: {cross} *Goring* {cross} *at* {cross} *Dannye* {cross} // {cross} *in Sussex* {cross}. 12mm. 0.72g.

Location: Sold at *Timeline Auctions* 21-22 February 2017, Lot 514.

UNKNOWN FINDSPOT or DATE of DISCOVERY

Date: c.1600-c.1700.

Description: Silver flat circular ring, rectangular in section. Inscribed on both faces in flowing italic script: *neer Sitterburn // In: Kent.* 18mm. 2.92g.

Location. Offered at *Timeline Auctions* 6-9 December 2016, Lot 1803.

Type B

SOMERSET or DEVON, UNKNOWN DATE of DISCOVERY

Date: c.1600-c.1700.

Description: Silver ring, circular in plan and D-shaped in section. The flat exterior face inscribed: Return To Rarpe Arnold.

Location: With finder (information courtesy of Brian and Patrick Read).

UNKNOWN FINDSPOT or DATE of DISCOVERY

Date: c.1500-c.1600.

Description: Silver ring, circular in plan and of unknown section. The flat exterior face inscribed in serifed capitals: {cross} PEREGRINE. 9.5mm. 0.68g.

Location: Sold at *Timeline Auctions* 2 December 2011, Lot 792.

UNKNOWN FINDSPOT or DATE of DISCOVERY

Date: c.1450-c.1600.

Description: Silver ring, circular in plan and of (presumably) D-shaped section. The flat exterior face inscribed in serifed letters: {four-pointed star} Earle of {three-pointed star} Rutland.

Discussion: The auction catalogue dates this to the mid-15th century on the basis of a presumed association with Edmund Plantagenet, Earl of Rutland (c.1443-60). This is probably because of the identification of the script as derivative black letter. This script could have been in usage much later and it is possible the vervel references a later Earl of Rutland, e.g. Thomas Manners (c.1488-1543).

Location: Sold at *Timeline Auctions* 2 December 2011, Lot 793.

UNKNOWN FINDSPOT or DATE of DISCOVERY

Date: c.1600-c.1700.

Description: Silver ring, circular in plan and of D-shaped section. The flat exterior face inscribed in italics: {six-pointed star} *of Woodrisen Co: NORFF:* 9.11mm. 0.56g.

Location: Sold at *Timeline Auctions* 15-16 March 2012, Lot 1111.

UNKNOWN FINDSPOT or DATE of DISCOVERY

Date: c.1550-c.1700.

Description: Silver ring, circular in plan and of unknown section. The flat exterior face inscribed in non-serifed capitals: T MARTIN. 12mm. 2.06g.

Location: Offered at *Timeline Auctions* 9-12 September 2015, Lot 888.

UNKNOWN FINDSPOT or DATE of DISCOVERY

Date: c.1600-c.1700.

Description: Silver ring, circular in plan and of rectangular section. The flat exterior face inscribed in italics: *Jacob·Dunne.* 9.80mm. 1.54g.

Location: Sold at *Timeline Auctions* 24-27 May 2016, Lot 1899.

UNKNOWN FINDSPOT or DATE of DISCOVERY

Date: c.1550-c.1650.

Description: Silver ring, circular in plan and of unknown section. The flat exterior face inscribed in serifed capitals: STAFORD {cross} FOVKES {cross}. 9.84mm. 0.95g.

Location: Offered at *Timeline Auctions* 21-22 February 2017, Lot 513.

Type Ci
UNKNOWN FINDSPOT or DATE of DISCOVERY

Date: c.1550-c.1650.

Description: Silver ring, circular in plan and D-shaped in section. The flat exterior face inscribed in serifed capitals: S·WILL·RUSSELL. Opposite the inscription, where the two ends of the ring meet, a shield-shaped plate is attached vertically with solder. Engraved on the face of the plate is an image of what appears to be a stag on a corse, *statant*. The surface of the plate is heavily worn. 10.30mm. 0.95g.

Location: Sold at *Timeline Auctions* 18 March 2011, Lot 833.

UNKNOWN FINDSPOT or DATE of DISCOVERY

Date: c.1550-c.1700.

Description: Silver ring, circular in plan and D-shaped in section. The flat exterior face inscribed in italics: *Chadwell:of:Nort* {cross}. Opposite the inscription, where the two ends of the ring meet, a shield-shaped plate is attached vertically with solder. The face of the plate is engraved with a coat of arms depicting a chevron between three hammers. 10mm. 1.17g.

Location: Sold at *Timeline Auctions* 5 October 2012, Lot 1299.

UNKNOWN FINDSPOT or DATE of DISCOVERY

Date: c.1550-c.1700.

Description: Silver ring, circular in plan and D-shaped in section. The flat exterior face inscribed in serifed capitals: W.PELLAM. Opposite the inscription, where the two ends of the ring meet, a shield-shaped plate is attached vertically. The face of the plate is engraved with a depiction of a buckle standing on a corse. 9.34mm. 1.41g.

Location: Sold at *Timeline Auctions* 3-4 September 2014, Lot 1029.

Type Cii
UNKNOWN FINDSPOT or DATE of DISCOVERY

Date: c.1550-c.1700.

Description: Silver ring, circular in plan and rectangular in section. The flat exterior face inscribed in serifed capitals: OF HITCHIN. Opposite the inscription, where the two ends of the ring meet, a shield-shaped plate is attached horizontally. The face of the plate is engraved with an image of a dexter hand surrounded at the wrist by a rope. On opposite sides of the hand the initials T and M are engraved. The border of the shield is highlighted by a toothed line. 8.71mm. 1.64g.

Location: Sold at *Timeline Auctions* 27-30 May, Lot 1626.

UNKNOWN FINDSPOT or DATE of DISCOVERY

Date: c.1550-c.1700.

Description: Silver ring, (presumably) circular in plan and of rectangular section. The flat exterior face inscribed in serifed capitals: N. ASHETON. Attached horizontally, opposite the inscription, is a shield-shaped plate. The plate is engraved with arms; it is divided per chevron with vertical lines above and a sword between two pellets below. 10mm. 1.41g.

Location: Sold at *Timeline Auctions* 9-12 September 2015, Lot 887.